ISLAMIC FOUNDATIONS OF A FREE SOCIETY

EDITED BY NOUH EL HARMOUZI AND LINDA WHETSTONE

with contributions from

MUSTAFA ACAR • SOUAD ADNANE
AZHAR ASLAM • HASAN YÜCEL BAŞDEMIR
KATHYA BERRADA • MASZLEE MALIK • YOUCEF MAOUCHI
HICHAM EL MOUSSAOUI • M. A. MUQTEDAR KHAN
BICAN ŞAHIN • ATILLA YAYLA

iea

Institute of
Economic Affairs

First published in Great Britain in 2016 by
The Institute of Economic Affairs
2 Lord North Street
Westminster
London SW1P 3LB
in association with London Publishing Partnership Ltd
www.londonpublishingpartnership.co.uk

The mission of the Institute of Economic Affairs is to improve understanding of the fundamental institutions of a free society by analysing and expounding the role of markets in solving economic and social problems.

A CIP catalogue record for this book is available from the British Library.

ISBN 978-0-255-36728-8

Many IEA publications are translated into languages other than English or are reprinted. Permission to translate or to reprint should be sought from the Director General at the address above.

Typeset in Kepler by T&T Productions Ltd
www.tandtproductions.com

Printed and bound in Great Britain by Hobbs the Printers Ltd

CONTENTS

THE AUTHORS

Mustafa Acar

Mustafa Acar is Professor of Economics at N. Erbakan University, Konya, Turkey. He received his BA from Middle East Technical University, Ankara (1986), his Masters (1996) and his PhD (2000) from Purdue University, all in economics. He was Departmental Chair and Dean at Kirikkale University, and Rector at Aksaray University. He has published extensively in national and international academic journals, authored 14 books, translated 12 books, and contributed 37 chapters in edited books.

Souad Adnane

Souad Adnane is a Fulbright alumna. She holds an MA in Public Policy with a focus on Women's Studies from the George Washington University. She is a co-founder and active member of the Arab Center for Scientific Research and Humane Studies, a classical liberal think tank based in Morocco. She is also a board member of the Istanbul Network for Liberty, whose mission is to explore the principles and values of a free society within the Muslim world. She worked for seven years in the development sector, with different international NGOs, coordinating projects aimed at the empowerment of women and vulnerable populations.

Azhar Aslam

Azhar Aslam is a founder member of the Istanbul Network for Liberty and chief executive of EO Vision 21 Foundation, a Pakistani-based NGO. He is the Program Director of its Speed Literacy Program, with a mission to eradicate illiteracy in Pakistan. He also writes on Islamic issues, including previously for the Institute of Economic Affairs.

Hasan Yücel Başdemir

Hasan Yücel Başdemir is Associate Professor of Islamic Philosophy at the Yildirim Beyazit University in Ankara, Turkey. He is a Board Member of the Association for Liberal Thinking (ALT) in Turkey, editor of Liberte Publications of ALT and coordinates ALT's Center for the Studies on Religion and Liberty. He has authored *Ethical Foundations of Liberalism* (Liberte, 2009) and *The Problem of Definition of Knowledge in Contemporary Epistemology* (Hitit Kitap, 2010), and edited *Religious Freedom and Laicism in Turkey* (Liberte, 2011). His research interests focus on Islamic political thought, freedom of religion, the links between ethics and politics, and comparative epistemology.

Kathya Berrada

Kathya Berrada is a research associate at the Arab Center for Scientific Research and Humane Studies, a Moroccan-based think tank. Before joining the Center, Kathya worked for rating agencies and consultancy firms in France, Belgium and Morocco. Kathya holds a Masters degree in business from Grenoble Graduate business School and is currently pursuing her PhD in economics.

Nouh El Harmouzi

Nouh El Harmouzi has a BA in business studies and a Masters and PhD in economics, the latter from the Université Paul Cézanne, where the topic of his thesis was *Beliefs, Institutions and Economic Dynamics: The Case of Arab-Muslim Countries*. He is an editor of www.minbaralhurriyya.org, the Arabic-language news and analysis website, and teaches part time at Ibn Toufail University in Kenitra, Morocco. Since 2013 he has been director of the first democrat-liberal think tank created in Morocco: the Arab Center for Scientific Research and Humane Studies (www.arab-csr.org).

Maszlee Malik

Maszlee Malik graduated from the Al al-Bayt University in Jordan in 1994 with a degree in the field of *fiqh* and *usul al-fiqh*. His master's degree in the same field is from the University of Malaya and he obtained his PhD in political science at Durham University. He is currently assistant professor in the Faculty of Islamic Revealed Knowledge and Human Sciences at the International Islamic University Malaysia, Kuala Lumpur.

Youcef Maouchi

Youcef Maouchi is the director of the Institute for Economic Studies, Europe. He holds a PhD in economics from Aix-Marseille Université, France. He was a teaching and a research fellow at Aix-Marseille Université and a regular lecturer on Islamic Finance at the Legal and Commercial Cooperation with the Arab World programme at the Aix-Marseille Law School and in economics at the Kedge Business School. He also worked as a research assistant for Atlas Network's francophone project UnMondeLibre.org.

Hicham El Moussaoui

Hicham El Moussaoui obtained his PhD in economics in 2008 at the Université Paul Cézanne (Aix-Marseille III). Since 2009, he has been Assistant Professor in Economics at Sultan Moulay Slimane University, Morocco. He joined the Atlas Foundation for Economic Research in 2008, where he is the editor of www.libreAfrique.org, a French-speaking project to defend ideas of freedom in Africa.

M. A. Muqtedar Khan

M. A. Muqtedar Khan is Associate Professor in the Department of Political Science and International Relations at the University of Delaware. He earned his PhD in International Relations, Political Philosophy and Islamic Political Thought, from Georgetown University in May 2000. He founded the Islamic Studies programme at the University of Delaware and was its first director from 2007 to 2010. Dr Muqtedar Khan is a fellow of the Institute for Social Policy and Understanding. He was a senior non-resident fellow of the Brookings Institution (2003–8) and a fellow of the Alwaleed Center at Georgetown University (2006–7). He has been the president, vice president and general secretary of the Association of Muslim Social Scientists.

Bican Şahin

Bican Şahin is an Associate Professor of Political Science at Hacettepe University, Ankara. He earned his PhD at the University of Maryland, College Park, US, in 2003. He is the President of the Freedom Research Association, a classical liberal think tank based in Ankara.

Linda Whetstone

Linda Whetstone is chairman of Network for a Free Society and a board member of the Atlas Network, Institute of Economic Affairs, the Mont Pelerin Society and the Istanbul Network for Liberty. She works with think tanks worldwide that promote markets, with a particular emphasis on those in mainly Muslim countries.

Atilla Yayla

Atilla Yayla is Professor of Social and Political Theory at Halic University, Istanbul, Turkey. He was a founder of the Association for Liberal Thinking, the first classical liberal intellectual movement in the Islamic World. He is head columnist of the Yeni Yuzyil daily newspaper.

FOREWORD

Throughout human history, religious leaders, philosophers, scholars, academics, community elders and ordinary citizens have tried to make a better world in which the human community can develop and flourish. They have done this in diverse ways, for example, through religion, philosophy, tradition and law. The prevention of despotism, totalitarianism, injustice and the abuse of the inherent rights of individuals has often been considered a priority by religions and most philosophers.

Throughout the history of Islamic societies the Sharia has formed the main framework of socio-economic and even the political life of the Islamic peoples. During the golden age of Islam (800–1200 AD) the Sharia always seemed compatible with a free society, and this was the experience of Muslim communities. The emergence of a pluralistic intellectual climate, the growth of several schools of thought in Islamic societies (theology and jurisprudence), scientific achievements in chemistry, medicine, agriculture, music, poetry, philosophy and astronomy, together with the development of commerce and trade, went hand-in-hand with Muslims engaging freely with non-Muslim societies. A robust context for the promotion and the protection of property rights in the light of the economic engagement of Muslims with other ancient traditions led to the establishment of well-respected and well-supported enterprises.

The legal and juridical principles of Islamic law recognised individual freedom and rights (along with the responsibilities of individuals) in a society that provided an appropriate context for an independent judiciary and the defence of individual rights through the courts. Islam insists on freedom of movement and, in principle, does not recognise boundaries between Islamic societies. Islam shared these characteristics with other progressive legal systems and religions in the world and it also promoted business and trade with all non-Muslims.

Muslims comprise a major segment of the human community, making up 23 per cent of the world's population clustered in 54 Islamic countries. There is a need to bring prosperity and greater welfare to Muslim societies. This will only happen if Muslims reflect on the golden age in their history when freedom and co-existence with other communities, including a pluralistic intellectual climate, existed and if they draw the right lessons from it. This comprehensive book is an excellent, unique and valuable initiative for intellectuals, civil society activists (including university students), journalists and ordinary people who want to understand the basic elements of a free society and their compatibility with Islamic traditions and thought. I am sure it will be very useful for those who promote freedom in countries where these principles are not well understood. I would particularly like to encourage its Muslim readers to read it carefully in order to develop their knowledge of Islamic principles, so that they can understand more clearly the consistency of free society values with Islamic Sharia. Furthermore, this book will be useful for non-Muslims who wish to understand the richness of Islamic thought, especially given the number of Muslims who live in Western countries and who are sometimes seen as a threat. As such, this book is being published at a vital time in world history and, if properly understood and promoted, can help bring about again a better world in which the human community can develop and flourish.

M. ABUL AHRAR RAMIZPOOR
Former lecturer at Kabul University and general co-ordinator of
the Afghanistan Economic and Legal Studies Organization (AELSO)
A founder of the Istanbul Network for a Free Society
Kabul, Afghanistan

April 2016

The views expressed in this monograph are, as in all IEA publications, those of the author and not those of the Institute (which has no corporate view), its managing trustees, Academic Advisory Council members or senior staff. With some exceptions, such as with the publication of lectures, all IEA monographs are blind peer-reviewed by at least two academics or researchers who are experts in the field.

ACKNOWLEDGEMENT

A number of chapters in this book were developed from presentations made at the annual conferences held by the Istanbul Network for Liberty, whose mission is to explore and promote the principles and values of a free society in the Muslim world (http://istanbulnetwork.org/).

TABLES, FIGURES AND BOXES

1 INTRODUCTION

Kathya Berrada and Nouh El Harmouzi

Abu-Bakr al-Baghdadi, the head of ISIS, announced himself as Caliph and a Commander of Believers at a mosque in Iraq in July 2014. Following this announcement, the terms 'Caliph', 'Caliphate' and 'Sharia law' have come under intense scrutiny in Western media. While those terms may seem alien in the West and sometimes associated with horror and violence, they are very familiar in the Muslim world. Indeed, these terms were initially used to describe the primary authorities in the theocratic Islamic states of the past. Theologically and historically, the term 'Caliph' refers to the Commander of Believers in an Islamic state (or Caliphate) vested with the responsibility to enforce the application of Sharia. In turn, Sharia is largely defined as a system of law determining Islamic duties from birth until death. Sharia ordinances are derived from the Quran, the tradition of the prophet, analogy and consensus.

Understanding and applying Sharia law is at the heart of a very important debate in the Islamic world, with conservative Muslims and jurists on one side and reformists on the other. Conservative jurists tend to view Sharia laws as a fixed set of divine rules that transcend time and space. It should be mentioned that despite the fact that conservative jurists are in favour of upholding Sharia, they generally oppose the use of violence in the pursuit of this goal while jihadi factions are in favour of using force and violence to establish a Caliphate with rigorous application of Sharia. Reformists, on the other hand, consider rules to be bound to their time and place and, as such, permanent ordinances and eternal rules are not conceivable. Reformists are also of the opinion that Sharia as we know it is not divine and is simply the understanding of Islamic sources of the past jurists with the specific historical consideration of their time and place. While most reformists think that laws cannot be permanent, they assert that values and moral norms can and, as such, call for an understanding of Sharia from a virtue perspective rather than a legal one.[1]

To be more nuanced, one should mention that the reformist movement within the Islamic world cannot be viewed as a monolithic group and that different views and understandings underline the work of various reformists. Furthermore, the reform movements are far from being a new phenomenon within the Islamic tradition. Averroes, the twelfth-century Andalusian jurist and philosopher, is one of the early Islamic figures who aimed to reform the dominant religious understanding of his time. Indeed, Averroes, referred to as 'the Commentator' by Saint Thomas Aquinas for his extensive commentaries on the work of Aristotle, is a crucial figure in understanding the intellectual battle fought by conservatives and reformists in the Muslim world. In complete opposition to the dominant views of his time, Averroes favoured reason and philosophy. According to Averroes, truths must be approached by means of rational analysis. While accepting revelation he attempted to harmonise religion with philosophy without obliterating their differences. Furthermore, Averroes believed that the Quran contained the highest truth while affirming that its words should not be taken literally.

---

1   Another division between Muslims, much referenced but little understood in the Western world, is that between Sunnis and Shiites. This is not directly relevant to our discussion, but because of the frequency with which it is raised, it is discussed in Box 1.

Box 1   The Sunni–Shiite division

The roots of the division between Sunni and Shiite Muslims trace back to early history and relate to the disagreement over the succession to the authority of the Prophet Muhammad. Indeed, a schism occurred when the Prophet Muhammad died in 632, leading to a dispute over his succession. This dispute materialised in the Battle of Siffin and intensified greatly after the Battle of Karbala in which the grandson of Prophet Muhammad, Hussein, and Hussein's household were killed.

Throughout the medieval era, hostility flared between Sunnis and Shiites and what started as a political dispute over succession translated into differences in jurisprudence and religious interpretations.

Today, the overwhelming majority of Muslims are Sunni while a significant minority of Muslims (about 10–15 per cent) are Shiites. The Shiites are mainly concentrated in Iran, Iraq, Azerbaijan, Lebanon, Bahrain and Yemen, but significant Shiite communities live throughout the Muslim world.

In the post-revolutionary uprisings in the Arab world, particularly in countries such as Iraq, Bahrain and the Kingdom of Saudi Arabia, the question of Sunni–Shiite hostility and rivalry has again resurfaced, claiming the lives of many from both sides. The fear of a 'Shiite crescent' has been expressed by officials of some Sunni majority countries. However, this fear of Shiite solidarity against Sunnis may not be proven to be founded as, in general, whether people are Sunnis or Shiites has never been the sole deciding factor in a person's political identity. Economic, social, nationalistic and tribal factors cannot be ignored and may be more detrimental to the region than the Sunni versus Shiite divide.

The struggle of Averroes in favour of philosophy and reason continued to be the struggle of numerous Muslim thinkers who at different times in history had their share of issues to address. In the nineteenth century, for instance, the work of the Egyptian thinker Rifa'a al-Tahtawi was mainly concerned with reconciling Islamic and Christian civilisations. His writings stressed the need to accept the changes inherent in modern societies. The work of al-Tahtawi had an important impact on the Islamic Modernism movement and, more specifically, on Muhammed Abduh. As an influential Muslim reformer, Abduh maintained that Islam encourages its followers to detach themselves from the interpretations of their ancestors and of old jurists and engage instead in active intellectual endeavour to keep up with changing times.

Different times and different challenges have given birth to a new generation of Islamic reformists in the twentieth and twenty-first centuries who have been able to use modern social science frameworks to analyse and challenge religious dogmas. Named by *Time* magazine as one of the 100 most influential people in the world in 2005, Abdolkarim Soroush definitely represents this new generation of Islamic reformists. His work is based on a clear distinction between 'religion' and our 'understanding of religion' and 'essential' and 'accidental' aspects of religion. Soroush is an active supporter of religious freedom as understood by the capacity to accept or reject a faith, a topic which continues to be very controversial around the Islamic world.

Echoing the work of reformists, civil society actors in the Muslim world have also engaged in serious efforts to move from theoretical frameworks of reform to more practical social and economic changes. A subject that has been a major concern for civil society actors in Muslim-majority countries is that of women's rights. Indeed, a conservative interpretation of Islam, together with tribal structures and mentalities, has had an adverse impact on the position of women in society. Thinkers, intellectuals and civil society actors across the Muslim world have been calling for a more liberal interpretation of religion allowing women to enjoy more active political, social and economic roles. The Nobel Prize winner Shirin Abadi is without doubt a key figure in the fight for women's rights both in her country, Iran, and throughout the Muslim world. Abadi affirms that it is not religion that binds women, but the selective dictates of those who wish them to be cloistered.

In addition to purely theological reforms and social changes, promoting economic freedom in Muslim-majority countries is key to encouraging development and improving the lives of hundreds of millions of people. Despite the fact that Islam is rather in favour of entrepreneurial activities, Muslim-majority countries do not generally rank high in international indices of economic freedom and competitiveness. Large, intrusive governments, interventionism, rigid legal frameworks and high taxes have had a negative impact on the economic performance of a number of Muslim countries.

Conservative interpretations of Islam and a large centralised state apparatus have adversely affected the way in which Muslims understand economic freedom. But this should not overshadow the work of early Muslim thinkers. Indeed, as early as the fourteenth century, the Muslim thinker Ibn Khaldun made the case for a free economy and freedom of choice. He is credited with having affirmed that to maximise both earnings and levels of satisfaction, a man should be free to perform whatever his gifts, talents, skills and abilities dictate. Furthermore, Ibn Khaldun made a strong case against any government attempt to confiscate or detrimentally affect in any way private property. Governments' arbitrary interference in man's property, according to Ibn Khaldun, reduces incentives. Indeed, he viewed expropriation as self-defeating for any government because it is a form of oppression, and oppression ruins society. The words of Ibn Khaldun resonate even more so today in the current economic context of Muslim countries.

Promoting a liberal understanding of Islam does not mean ignoring a rich Islamic tradition of philosophy, thinking and jurisprudence. The spirit of the intellectual Islamic tradition can be celebrated while opening up the field for new ideas. In a letter addressed to the monks of St. Catherine's Monastery in Mt. Sinai, the Prophet Muhammad granted a Charter of Privileges, including clauses covering aspects of human rights, protection of Christians, freedom of worship and movement, freedom to appoint their own judges and freedom to own and maintain their property and the right to protection in war. It is, indeed, such a spirit that needs to be revived and granted permission to flourish in the light of the modern concepts of universal human rights and democracy that are prevalent in many modern states.

The contributions of the authors

Reviving an Islamic spirit while accepting the desire to adapt to modern times is a necessity, especially in this challenging context in which Islam is often associated with violence, terrorism and backwardness. This book is an attempt by a group of Muslim scholars to promote a liberal understanding of Islam. The writers explore concepts related to economics, women's rights, the meaning of jihad and other related topics.

Terms such as 'Islamic state' and 'Caliphate' have become widely used in different media and their ambiguous use leads us to reflect on a profound question: can Islam as a religion be separate from politics and be compatible with economic, social and political freedom?

As suggested by the authors of the second chapter of this book, Atilla Yayla and Bican Şahin, there are two answers to this question, an Islamist answer and a liberal Muslim answer. According to the first approach, Islam is a comprehensive system that encompasses both the private and public domains and, as such, Islam cannot be dissociated from politics. This view rejects personal choice and its equivalent in the political sphere, namely democracy. A state based on such an understanding controls every aspect of life and leaves no space for civil liberty, pluralism and minority rights.

The second and more enlightened answer comes from liberal Muslims, who either assert that, in essence, Islam and a liberal democratic order are compatible or that Islam is at least to a great extent silent on matters related to the life of the Muslim community. Atilla Yayla and Bican Şahin note that the first approach came to be more dominant in the Islamic world. While Islamic civilisation flourished when it developed a dialogue with other existing civilisations, it declined when it became secluded. Sometimes, a sense of political and economic inferiority in comparison with Western countries has made Muslims cling to an identity often derived from religion and to reject other world views. Historical factors have also contributed to this intellectual sclerosis, as suggested by Mustafa Acar in the third chapter of this book. One historical political factor identified by Acar is the Mongol invasion of the Muslim world in the thirteenth century. Another factor was the failure of the Innovationists-Rationalists in their battle against the Traditionalists in medieval times. This is indeed a well-documented clash between two mindsets and two different perspectives or mentalities, which could be named as *Ahl al-Ra'y* and *Ahl al-Hadith*.

There is no quick fix for this situation. Atilla Yayla and Bican Şahin make the case for adopting dynamic interpretations of Islam and addressing contemporary problems. They also stress the need to create a system within which individuals and groups who subscribe to different world views can live together in peace and harmony. Mustafa Acar, on the other hand, emphasises the need to go back to the history of Islamic thought, reread and rethink the debates.

It is indeed from this rereading of Islamic thought that Maszlee Malik in Chapter 4 proposes a rather original understanding of 'welfare beyond the state'. In what Malik refers to as the 'benevolent society' individuals are politically and economically less dependent on the state, but interdependent on each other as they relate to one another on the basis of mercy and justice. Indeed, *zakat* (the provision of charity) and *waqf* (land, property or cash used for charitable purposes) can be cited as insignia of Islamic welfare based on community solidarity and a minimal state. While both zakat and waqf existed in the early Islamic era, the author of this chapter calls for their appropriate readjustment to modern times. As such, waqf is to be understood within a larger and more dynamic framework far from the current exclusively ritual-spiritual-based paradigm. A non-state welfare system is, according to the author, capable of reinforcing individual responsibility.

This notion of individual responsibility is indeed crucial for the development of any society. Nevertheless, it should be mentioned that Muslim societies are perceived as collectivist and this is often mentioned as one of the reasons behind the failure of Muslims to adapt to modernity.

In the fifth chapter of the book, Azhar Aslam addresses the question of individual freedom of choice and its relationship with Islamic teachings. The author points out that, according to the Quran for example, on the day of judgement, the consequences of our earthly actions (in the form of reward or punishment) are specific to the individual. As such, no one is responsible for anyone else's actions. Responsibility also presupposes freedom of choice, without which any judgement becomes arbitrary. If the Quran is rather explicit in proposing individual freedom of choice, how can we explain the denial of the exercise of this freedom? The punishment for apostasy is often referred to as the most severe violation of a person's freedom to choose or reject the Islamic religion. Azhar Aslam explains, however, that the punishment for apostasy is not inherent to Islamic teachings. Rather, the punishment developed within a political context in which Islam was no longer understood as a value system that promoted justice and freedom.

Women's rights form another important set of issues that needs to be taken seriously in the Muslim world. In the sixth chapter, Souad Adnane affirms that socio-cultural and religious norms affect the position of women in the Muslim world. In this regard, the author refers to the patriarchal nature of the Middle East and North Africa (MENA), which are societies characterised by segregation between the 'private' and the 'public' that frames and forges gender roles. Religious interpretations are often used to justify cultural practices and to shape people's perceptions. This is clearly translated into a lack of participation in the political and economic spheres. Indeed, the MENA region records the world's lowest rate of female labour market participation (25 per cent compared with a global average of 50 per cent). However, Souad Adnane emphasises that Islam, as such, does not restrict women's participation in the economic life of the community and that no authorisations are required for women to engage in commercial transactions. The author makes the case for the importance of promoting economic freedom of women in the Arab world as a way to advance their status and also promote general economic growth. While the author argues that market-friendly policies promote the economic participation of women, she clearly stresses that their impact is limited if they are not gender sensitive and if nothing is done to address socio-cultural norms and structural inequalities.

Socio-economic considerations and narrow religious interpretations are also used to justify violence in the pursuit of political objectives in the Muslim world. Muqtedar Khan, in Chapter 7, argues for another narrative. According to the author, the Quran makes a strong case for forgiveness and for peace. It also does not permit the use of force against those who do not themselves use it. The value of peace is clear in the message of the Quran as it is introduced as the desired path in life as well as a value or reward for righteousness. Furthermore, the Quran forbids Muslims from initiating or perpetuating violence except in self-defence or to fight persecution.

The 'violence rhetoric' is also addressed in Chapter 8. Indeed, Hasan Yücel Başdemir explains that the emergence of such rhetoric is largely explained by rather historical factors and is far from being inherent to the Islamic religion. In this regard, the author notes that the institution of the Caliphate emerged as a result of the need of the Muslim people for earthly leadership and was not proposed by the Prophet. Nevertheless, literalist interpretations of Islam suggest that the Caliphate is the only political institution compatible with Islamic law. Therefore, what was historically constructed became understood by Muslims as a divinely prescribed model. In addition to this misconception, colonisation, followed by secular dictatorships in many Muslim countries, has strengthened jihadi movements. The author of the chapter asks an important question: in what kind of societies do Muslims aspire to live? The answer to this question will have a large impact on the lives of millions of people in Muslim-majority countries.

Moving on to Chapter 9 of the book, Hicham El Moussaoui makes the case for the compatibility of Islam with a market economy. El Moussaoui stresses the fact that Islam is very much in favour of work and productive effort to make legal profit. He also emphasises that the Quran seeks to reform society by reforming the individual. Indeed, Islam appeals to morality and not to coercion. In Islam, the notion of freedom extends to work, property and the choice of how to use one's capabilities and resources. Furthermore, Islam preserves free choice by limiting the scope of state intervention. While forbidding monopolistic power, Islam encourages competition by limiting state control over prices. The Prophet was equally sensitive to the rights of the sellers and he was against price-fixing even at times of scarcity. However, despite teachings and Islamic principles that are very much in favour of a market economy, the author notes that clear deviations from those principles exist in Muslim-majority countries due to, among other factors, misinterpretation of the religion, colonisation and socialist orientations of those in power.

Islamic finance is another topic related to economics and is examined in Chapter 10. Islamic finance can be understood as the conduct of financial transactions in a way that is compatible with Islamic teachings. At the heart of Islamic finance, we find different types of contracts at the base of a range of complex financial tools that can be classified into two groups: debt-like contracts and equity contracts. It is often mentioned within the industry that the difference between Islamic and conventional finance is not just a matter of banned interest or forbidden investments in *haram* industries. Advocates of Islamic finance aim to build a form of finance distinguishable from conventional finance by its entrepreneurial approach and use of investment and partnership tools. The author of the chapter recalls that the most powerful argument used by the proponents of Islamic finance is the idea of linking the financial sector to the real sector.

However, the author, Youcef Maouchi, notes that the reality of the Islamic finance industry does not match the underlying ideals. According to his analysis, after four decades, Islamic finance has fallen short of offering a substantive alternative to conventional finance. Nevertheless, it is clear that Islamic bankers have succeeded in developing a new industry within the financial landscape. Islamic finance is attracting new players. Muslims and non-Muslims alike are more attracted to the financial prospects and outlook of Islamic finance than they are to a totally new and different financial system.

The authors of this book do contemporary debate a great service. They help clarify understanding among Muslims of aspects of their own faith and how the tenets of their faith relate to the political world. Secondly, this book should help Westerners better understand Islamic thinking, which is often dismissed as reactionary and hostile. Given current debates, as well as the hostility and violence of religious groups in many parts of the world, *Islamic Foundations of a Free Society* is an especially timely contribution.

2 THE CONDITION OF SOCIAL, POLITICAL AND ECONOMIC THINKING IN THE ISLAMIC WORLD FROM A CLASSICAL LIBERAL PERSPECTIVE

Atilla Yayla and Bican Şahin

Freedom, religion and Islam

In his seminal essay 'Two Concepts of Liberty', Isaiah Berlin (1969) makes a twofold distinction between negative and positive liberty. According to the negative conception, persons are free to the extent to which they are not interfered with by others. In this understanding, freedom means the absence of coercion so that people can conduct their lives in their own way. Freedom provides a person with a private sphere in which the person is considered free regardless of the content of their decisions. In order for persons to be free, their decisions and/or actions do not need to serve an idealised lifestyle. The only criterion is that they must not harm other individuals.

According to the positive understanding of liberty, it is not enough that a person be free from external coercion. Free persons must also have the means to realise their life plans. Unless a person has necessary material resources, according to this view freedom from external interference, i.e. negative liberty, does not mean much. Furthermore, in order for a person to be free in the positive sense, that person's decisions and/or actions in life must meet certain ideal standards. In the first place, these decisions and actions must be taken by the rational self. They should reflect the true interest of the person. Decisions based on unexamined views or desires do not lead to freedom in the positive sense. In other words, a person is free only when free from both external/ physical constraints and inner/psychological constraints. The positive conception of liberty can be used by both non-religious and religious minded persons. For a non-religious individual, for example, persons can be said to be free when they are able to resist the temptations of consumerist culture. Thus, a person is not free in this sense if he desires to buy the latest iPhone even though he has the previous version in good condition. For a religious person who subscribes to a positive conception of liberty, a person is free when he follows the eternal truth and can resist the temptations of earthly pleasures. If a person gives in to temptation, he loses his freedom and would be a slave of his desires.

Using these two different conceptions of liberty, we can envisage two different sorts of free or liberal world. In the first kind, based on the negative conception of liberty, we can have a world in which there is room for lifestyles based on a negative as well as a positive conception of liberty. In this world, the responsibility of the state is limited to ensuring that individuals are not interfered with from outside. The state does not judge whether a person's decisions and/or actions are living up to certain ideals: it is up to individuals to determine what kind of life they will lead. In such a world, there is room for lifestyles that are based on the liberal concept of autonomy as well as for more traditional lifestyles. In the second sort of free or liberal society, which depends on the positive conception of liberty, individuals are expected to lead a particular kind of life. In this sort of free or liberal world, all individuals are supposed to lead liberal lives mostly based on the concept of autonomy, which requires constant rational evaluation of alternatives.

It would seem that the former type of liberal world, based on a negative conception of liberty, is likely to be more tolerant towards religion in the sense that it accommodates religious lifestyles more easily. Stated differently, religion that emphasises positive liberty in its essence does not have to be an enemy of a society organised on the principle of negative liberty. There is a difference between positive freedom exercised as an ethical doctrine and the adoption of positive freedom as the basis for the organisation of the state.[1] A political system based on a negative understanding of liberalism can accommodate religious ways of life as long as these religious views accept one particular liberal value, individual freedom of conscience (Kukathas 2003).

The ability or the faculty that shows us what is right and what is wrong in conducting our lives can be defined as conscience. In Adam Smith's language, it is 'the man within our breast' that constantly warns us against acting contrary to what we believe to be right. When we listen to and follow this voice, we feel rectitude or integrity; and when we do the contrary we feel remorse. The weakness of willpower or some external factors such as physical and/or psychological constraint may be the reason behind our failure to obey the dictates of our conscience. Regardless of the fact that we follow or fail to follow our conscience in practice, we believe that we should follow it at all times. Thus, the possession of a conscience forms the distinctive feature of human beings. In this respect, the fundamental interest of human beings is that they be able to lead a life in accordance with the dictates of their conscience. This corresponds to liberty of conscience. Regardless of their beliefs individuals have a primary interest in living a life according to their conscience. If the proposition that the fundamental interest of human beings is the ability to lead a life in accordance with the dictates of conscience is true, then what we need is negative freedom or toleration (Şahin 2010).

A free or liberal world that is based on a particular interpretation of positive freedoms, i.e. liberal autonomy, on the other

---

1   For further reading on the distinction between political and ethical/comprehensive versions of liberalism, see Waldron (2004).

hand, presents a world which may not accommodate some lifestyles that are based on different understandings of positive freedom (for example, some religious ways of life). In other words, this conceptualisation of freedom takes liberalism as an ethical doctrine and, as a result, it can accommodate only those ethical views that subscribe to that particular liberal way of life. This understanding inevitably conflicts with some forms of religion.[2]

Can Islam as a religion be separate from politics?

With regard to religion and its relationship to the public sphere, the crucial question that needs to be answered is whether religion is an ethical or a political system, or both. At the theoretical level, we can say that, if it is only an ethical system that prescribes for its followers a certain way of life, then it can exist in a free or liberal world based on political liberalism. But if a religion is both an ethical and a political system in which the particular ethical view should be enforced through political means, then even the free or liberal world based on a negative conception of liberty cannot accommodate it. The answer to the question of whether Islam is solely an ethical system or is both an ethical and a political system will also determine whether or not Islam is compatible with a free or liberal world. Simply put, there are two answers to this question: an Islamist answer and a liberal Muslim answer.

Islamists are those who believe that Islam provides believers with not only an ethical system on the basis of which they will achieve happiness in this world and in the life hereafter but also a political system through which the moral principles of Islam will be enforced. According to Islamists, there is no division

---

2   For example, an approach to positive freedom that has as one of its precepts the belief that all should receive the same level of state schooling to try to equalise opportunities is likely to lead to a situation where families' freedom to educate their children is restrained.

between the private and the public domains within Islam. This view rejects personal choice and its equivalent in the political sphere, i.e. democracy. One prominent Islamist from the Indian subcontinent, Sayyid Abu'l-A'la Maududi (1903–79) (1985: 30), puts this point very succinctly: 'In [an Islamic] state, no one can regard any field of his affairs as personal and private'. Another well-known Islamist, Sayyid Qutb (1906–66) from Egypt, parallels Maududi by stating: '[I]f it is asked "Should not the interest of individuals shape their existence?", then we must refer once again to the question and answer at the heart of Islam: "Do you know or does God know?" "God knows and you do not know"' (quoted by Tripp 1994: 169).

As Vali Nasr (2005: 16) argues, 'Islamist ideology ... calls for the creation of a utopian Islamic state that notionally vests all sovereignty in God. This call is based on a narrow interpretation of Islamic law, and promotes an illiberal, authoritarian politics that leaves little room for civil liberties, cultural pluralism, the rights of women and minorities, and democracy.' In this sense, it is not misleading to say that Islamism is a comprehensive ideology that combines the ethical and political worlds, and the state, which is based on this ideology, controls every aspect of life (Qutb 1953; Maududi 1985). To the extent that Islamist scholars such as Maududi and Qutb extinguish the division between the public and private and make the personal subordinate to the common, Islamism can even be seen as a form of totalitarianism (Esposito 1998) and thus incompatible with a free or liberal world.[3]

In our presentation of the liberal Muslim answer we will follow Leonard Binder's (1988) analysis. Binder makes a distinction

---

3 Even Maududi (1985) himself accepts the fact that the Islamic state he defends resembles the fascist and communist states in this respect. However, he believes that, even though the Islamic state is an all-inclusive state, it is completely different from the modern totalitarian and authoritarian states (page 30). For Maududi, what makes Islamic totalitarianism a good form of totalitarianism, and totally different from the modern totalitarianisms, is the fact that it is based on God's orders (Esposito 1998: 153).

between two sorts of *Islamic liberalism* or *liberal Islam* (pages 24–44), although, for different reasons, both of these approaches argue that Islam and a free or liberal democratic order are compatible. In the first branch of Islamic liberalism there are two justifications for a liberal democratic political system in a Muslim society. Firstly, a liberal democratic system is in accordance with the general spirit of Islam, which is tolerant of diversity as witnessed by the Prophet Muhammad's statement, '[d]ifference of opinion within my community is a sign of God's mercy'. Secondly, Islam is to a great extent silent regarding the political organisation of the society of Muslims. Thus, in the absence of any specific rules, except for the institution of *shura* (consultation) regarding political matters, this first group of Islamic liberals argue, Muslims can choose a liberal democratic political order over alternative political arrangements.

However, for the second branch of Islamic liberalism, specific references to Islam form the main pillar of argument in favour of the compatibility of Islam and a liberal democratic order. These liberal Muslims refer to 'explicit legislation such as the Quranic provision for taking counsel, or the denial of the sovereign authority of man over man, or the Sharia (Islamic law) provisions for "electing" the Caliph (Islamic leader), or the Hadith (the acts and sayings of the Prophet Muhammed) concerning the equality of believers' (Binder 1988: 244). As one of the representatives of this second approach puts it: '[l]iberal Islam is a branch, or school, of Islam that emphasizes human liberty and freedom within Islam' (Masmoudi 2003: 40). Hence, these liberal Muslims start with one of the basic teachings of Islam: 'there can be no compulsion in religion'. The cornerstones of this second version of Islamic liberalism are: *hurriya* (liberty), *adl* (justice), *shura* (consultation) and *ijtihad* (rational interpretation) (Masmoudi 2003).

Although the liberal Muslim view is compatible with a liberal democratic order, this is not the dominant view in the Muslim world. Rather, the Islamist view is more widespread. In what follows we examine the reasons for this and attempt to make a case for liberal values within Islamic social, economic and political thinking.

The current situation of social, political and economic thought in Islamic countries

This part of the chapter does not aim or claim to bring definite solutions to the problems that have been discussed for decades or even centuries. However, we hope that it will shed some light on various methodological problems and identify several mistakes that have distorted the way Muslims think about them. It will also propose some areas where further study is necessary to make progress in meeting contemporary needs and demands.

It is not wrong to say that the Islamic world as a whole is in a desperately bad position in many respects. To understand how bad the situation is, we can compare the Islamic world today with the Islamic world towards the end of the first millennium. In the last centuries of the first millennium, the Islamic world was much more advanced than any other part of the world, including Europe or what we today call the West. This was true in science, medicine and the economy, as well as tolerance and peaceful co-existence (Koechler 2004). That situation has been completely reversed. The Islamic world is now poor in both absolute and relative terms. Muslims fail to enjoy basic human rights in many Islamic lands. They often suffer under oppressive regimes led by non-religious or religious dictators.

Why did this happen? There are several explanations. Some claim that Islam as a religion is not and can never be compatible with civilisation; that it rejects all the values that created civilisation and has a natural tendency to create terrorism. Those who believe that Islamic teachings feed terrorism easily become Islamophobic and see an actual or potential terrorist in every Muslim person. Interestingly, there are also subscribers to this approach in the Islamic countries themselves. These people have attempted from time-to-time to colonise their countries and peoples on behalf of anti-Islamic ideas and powers.

Islamists think that the reason for the backwardness of Islamic countries is the attempt by Muslim peoples to imitate the West. In doing so, Muslims distanced themselves from superior Islamic values, which caused them to fall behind the West. They believe that the solution is to reject all Western values and turn to the robust, untouched, holy essence of the Islamic religion. This is the belief of the Salafi movements or Islamic fundamentalists. A milder version of this approach proposes that Muslims should benefit from the science and technology of the West but, at the same time, keep away from Western culture and morality, or rather the lack of it.

If we leave aside such explanations, we can identify several sociological and historical reasons why the Islamic world lagged behind the West. First comes the Mongol occupation of the Islamic world and the destruction of the administrative, educational, scientific and cultural structure (Roskin and Coyle 2008: 35). Certainly, the Mongols also caused a loss of self-confidence among Muslims. Then comes the discovery of the new transportation routes which bypassed the Islamic lands to reach the West and Far East. This caused further destruction in commercial culture and activity. These events contributed to the absolute and relative backwardness of the Islamic world. However, from a classical liberal standpoint, another equally important factor is the inability of the intellectual classes in the Islamic world to develop ideas on which to base a free and prosperous society.

To put it more clearly, there have been no Islamic counterparts of Adam Smith, John Locke, J. S. Mill and F. A Hayek in Muslim countries. We come across strong and profound authors on literature in the Islamic world, but no thinker who has been able to produce, or even tried to produce, a theory of politics and economics. We have among others Ibn Khaldun (1322–1406), Khayrettin

Pasha (1822–90), Ottoman author Namık Kemal (1840–88) and Egyptian theologian 'Ali 'Abd al-Raziq (1888–1966), who all proclaimed some rudimentary ideas towards a full-fledged theory of political economy.[4] However, none of them, unfortunately, developed any sophisticated theory that can be compared with those that came into existence in the West. The Islamic political literature lacks very important concepts too. There is no counterpart of the terms 'limited state', 'constitutionalism', 'universal human rights' and 'citizenship' in major Islamic languages. In Islamic political literature, calls are made to sultans inviting them to be fair and just and to respect human beings; but no definite principles and theories exist on which to construct an open, transparent and participatory political system.

The same is true for economic literature in the Islamic world. The most obvious part of Islamic thinking that is well known is the rejection of interest. But this is not unique to Muslims and does not mean what it is commonly held to mean. Many philosophers, such as Aristotle in ancient Greece, were against interest, and Christianity also rejected it. Secondly, the rejection and condemnation of interest does not help much in devising an economic theory. There is no systematic work in the Islamic thought tradition on consumer behaviour, firm patterns, capital formation, saving and investment, money, banking, micro- and macroeconomic theory. The lack of ideas, or the failure to develop new ideas, concepts and theories that successfully answer the needs of humanity in every field is among the main causes of the backwardness of the Islamic world, rather than the rejection of interest as such. Certainly Islam does not prohibit long-term financing in ways that share risks appropriately and so there is no intrinsic barrier to the development of a sophisticated economy. But, there is little Islamic thinking in this area. If

---

4   'Ali 'Abd al-Raziq (1998) challenged the conviction that the religious and political leadership could unite in one person as proven by the experience of prophet Muhammad (see also Fialali-Ansary 2002: 245).

ideas have consequences, then a poverty of ideas must also have consequences. The situation in the Islamic world can be seen as evidence of the negative effect of the lack of ideas.

This raises the question, why did this happen? An answer to this question offered by some writers is that it related to the closing of ijtihad, which is the production of new ideas with respect to the interpretation of Islamic sources (Masmoudi 2002). There appears to be a widespread consensus among Muslim and non-Muslim scholars that the so-called ijtihad door was closed centuries ago and, because of this, Muslims could not develop new ideas or make interpretations of basic Islamic principles to meet new circumstances.

This is only partly true. By the failure to develop new ideas we do not mean only the failure to reinterpret Islamic principles stated in the Quran and other sources of Islam. Furthermore, we cannot be sure that the reopening of the door to ijtihad can and will solve this problem. There is a much broader problem in Islamic political, social and economic thinking because something more than the ending of ijtihad happened to the Muslim mind. The Muslim mind moved from being an open mind to being a closed mind that completely rejects the outside world and other ideas in favour of Muslim political entities and ideas (Rokeach 1960). Thus, it is synonymous with dogmatism. It produces intolerance and exclusion. In the Islamic world the advent of the closed mind has been helped, interestingly but not surprisingly, by both the feeling of inferiority in economic and military power and the sense of superiority in culture and morality.

In contrast to the first millennium, the Islamic world turned in towards itself in the second half of the second millennium and developed a reactionary attitude, especially against the West. In the first millennium, ancient Greek philosophy that faced the danger of completely disappearing from the world was saved by the Muslims. Europe rediscovered it partly through translations from Arabic. Many Europeans such as Albertus Magnus, Roger

Bacon, Thomas Aquinas and William of Ockham developed their intellectual skills in Arabic-Islamic universities in Cordoba, Sevilla, Granada, Valencia and Toledo (Koechler 2004). There was self-confidence in the Islamic lands then; Muslims saw the whole accumulation of human knowledge as their own.

Towards the middle of the second millennium this great self-confidence and inner peace was overtaken by a sense of helplessness and vulnerability towards the West. The Muslim world turned in on itself. The line of thought that the Muslims used in justifying this new, unprecedented attitude was as follows: 'the West might be more advanced in science, technology, and much stronger in economic and military structure; but it is undoing itself in culture and morals. The West has collapsed or it is about to collapse. We are superior to Christians due to our values, beliefs, and social culture.'

Under these circumstances, social and political thought in Islamic lands lost its original trajectory. The negative attitude and closed minds of the intellectual leaders started repeating previously produced thoughts within a vicious circle, instead of trying to develop new and progressive ideas. Those who read Islam's history know that Islam started as a revolutionary religion. It rejected inequalities and privileges that came by birth. It criticised women's second-class status in social affairs, bringing important rights for them, and even saved the lives of many newborn girls (Akyol 2011). Islam, in the beginning, fought against political oppression on the basis of religion and solved various social problems. Islam declared that human beings could not be slaves to other human beings; that all human beings were equal; it recognised and protected private property; and Islam promoted free trade. Islam was the only religion espoused by a merchant and the Muslim community was founded in a commercial society (Sorman 2011).

All those beliefs had indicated a certain direction for the Muslim world and, if history had not changed, Muslims could have continued on that trajectory. In other words, Muslims should have made a teleological reading of the Islamic sources and early history of Islam and should have continued with this. Unfortunately, that is not what happened. Islamic thought first stopped progressing in its original direction and then rolled back. The result is there for all to see.

What are the most basic errors in Muslim thought now and how can they be changed?

1. Muslim thinkers tend to treat some other Muslims and non-Muslims, specifically Christian Westerners, as if they were a different species. This is nonsense. We are human beings before being Muslim or non-Muslim, white or black, male or female. We have common needs and experiences in life and there will be things Muslims can and should learn from the experiences and thought of non-Muslims. Otherwise, they have closed minds.

2. The basic sources of Islam including from the time of prophet Muhammed must be subject to teleological interpretations. Muslims should progress in the original direction that the Quran and prophet Muhammed indicated. They should not behave as if history has ended; and instead of making static repetitions they need to adopt dynamic interpretations and address contemporary problems.

3. There is no doubt that Muslims have to read, understand and follow the Quran and the Sunna. However, this is not enough to understand the full and true nature of the human world. For a Muslim, Allah is the creator of the whole world and of all human beings. If there are rules embedded into the nature of individual and social life, they must have been created by Allah. Therefore Muslims must try to discover and express them. In other words, if the Quran is the small book of Allah, nature and the whole

human world is the big book of Allah. It is a duty for Muslims to read both books.

4. Some writers claim that Muslims should go back to the origins of the Quran and clear it from tradition and history. This is an impossible mission. The Quran does not speak on its own. It is given voice by Muslims and each Muslim understands it within his or her conditions and capacity. There is no other way. If it were possible to free a general interpretation of the Quran completely from traditions and history, that interpretation itself becomes in time tradition and history. So it is unrealistic to claim that the Quran must be cleared from previous traditions and interpretations. What is needed in the Islamic world is not an interpretation that is free of tradition and history but freedom that allows Muslims to make different and competing interpretations.

5. A concept of natural law needs to be developed within Islamic social and political thinking. It can be developed by studying the big book of Allah. In Western liberal tradition, a natural law concept, both in its religious and secular forms, played a very important role in overcoming dogmatism and fanaticism.

6. The general concept of human rights must also be defended in the Islamic world. This concept refers to human beings as subjects who have basic, inalienable, indispensable rights regardless of sex, ethnicity and religion. Human rights theory has done a lot to weaken religious and secular fanaticism in the West. The same might happen in the Islamic world.

In order to launch a general theory of human rights, Muslims must again read the big book of Allah. Instead of devising a general theory of human rights, some attempted to build a concept of 'Islamic human rights'. This might help Muslims embrace human rights, but does not create a general framework within which a broader understanding can find a place and all can be comfortable. Human rights founded on any religion, Muslim or Christian, are bound to be sectarian and discriminatory. Because of this we need a universal concept of human rights in the Islamic culture.

7. Muslim thought also needs a general concept of the individual. In fact Islam in its first decades empowered the individual against tribalism. The Quran defined man as 'God's viceroy on the earth', before which time tribes and tribalism were supreme. Prior to Islam, the penal system recognised the tribe, not the individual, as subject and the Quran changed this understanding (Akyol 2011). Unfortunately, in the following decades collectivism captured Islamic thinking. If so-called Islamic human rights say that only Muslims can have human rights, it cannot be a universal human rights theory and a general theory of constitutional government cannot be constructed out of this concept.

8. Muslims have mostly failed to understand the real nature and implications of freedom. Many of them subscribe to a kind of positive freedom: inner freedom. In this approach it is believed that one is free if one obeys Allah's orders regarding what to do and what not to do. This conceptualisation implies that only Muslims can enjoy freedom. In other words, being Muslim comes first and freedom comes only with Muslimness. This is wrong. It takes freedom as something that is linked with the relations between the individual and God. Freedom has nothing to do with relations between an individual and God; it is concerned with relations between individuals; it is a social product. Being a human is a general human condition while being Muslim or Christian or atheist refers to a specific human condition. People cannot be free by believing or not believing in a religion and practising its requirements, but they can adopt a religion if they have freedom. In Islamic culture those who are unfree cannot be considered to be responsible for their deeds. One who is not free cannot be a

real Muslim. However, free persons do not have to choose Islam as their religious belief, which means that in any given country everybody must have the right to enjoy freedom if Muslims really are to be free.

We can clarify further what freedom means and how it relates to a believer's relationship with Allah. In Islam there is a holy ban on alcohol consumption. Drinking alcohol is a sin, an action human beings have the capacity to commit, but which is forbidden by Allah. Some Muslims think that Muslims become free by obeying God. This interpretation is right in the sense that Muslim believers become alcohol-free. However, being alcohol-free is not the same as being free. If it were, then those who do not believe in the Muslim God would also not be free since they do drink alcohol. The problem in this strange situation results from confusing the legitimate field of freedom-related discussions with religious ones. If one is free, one has the right to drink or not drink alcohol. If one is forced by somebody else (but not by God) to drink or not to drink alcohol, one is not free. Thus freedom comes first and individuals have the right to make choices if they are free. In the case of alcohol consumption, both those who drink alcohol and those who do not can be free.[5]

9. A big problem in the Islamic world is the obsession with the idea of an Islamic state. Many Muslims demand an Islamic state instead of limited, constitutional government because they believe they can only have freedom if they live in such an Islamic state. This approach harms the freedom of non-Muslims and Muslims alike. In order to be free and to lead an Islamic life, what

---

5   There is a potential confusion of language here because of different meanings of the word 'freedom', the existence of which very much illustrates the importance of greater scholarship in this area. In a theological sense, we can say that we are 'free' if we are not a 'slave' to alcohol. However, if we do not drink simply because we are compelled not to drink, that decision has not been reached freely. People should have the economic and political freedom to make choices and come, without coercion, to choose what is right.

a Muslim needs is not an Islamic state, but a limited and constitutional government. Muslims cannot enjoy freedom while other human beings are unfree (Başdemir 2010).

10. Muslims should rid themselves of the simultaneous sense of inferiority and superiority in respect of the West. History is not limited to a few centuries; it is a long, incessant process. There is no guarantee that those who are inferior today will not be superior tomorrow. Things can change. Besides, our current understanding of basic human rights and values is not the product of any single culture or religion, but a common product of all humanity. Freedom of belief and expression, the right to private property, the right for equal recognition, belong to all human beings. It is wrong to attach them to any specific culture or religion, be it Western culture, Christianity or Islam.

The revolts against dictators in Muslim Arab countries raised hopes that the peoples of Islamic countries could have freedom under limited and constitutional government. Whether or not these hopes will be realised remains to be seen. In this context, some commentators are making comparisons between Turkey and North African Arab countries, arguing that Turkey succeeded in transforming itself from a single-party regime into a kind of limited democracy much earlier due to Mustafa Kemal Atatürk's reforms. It is true that Turkey moved to democracy from dictatorship several decades ago. It happened in 1950 with almost no violence. However, this was not due to the efforts of a single-party dictatorship and its policies and reforms. Rather, it happened despite them.

The Turkish spring in 1950 was a rejection of many political arrangements that belonged to the single-party government era. What changed in Turkey in the 1950s? Between 1925 and 1950 Turkey had a single-party system that did not allow opposing political parties and free elections: there was no political competition. The government elected itself with no real participation from the public. Turkey lacked freedom of religion and con-science, freedom of thought and expression, the rule of law, and an independent and impartial judiciary. There was no effective protection for private property. There was, and still is, the un-questionable personality cult of the supreme political leader. Turkey became the subject of one of the wildest attempts at cultural revolution in world history. The alphabet was changed without seeking the general consent of the citizens; the state promulgated dress codes in the society; the Kurdish language was forbidden; different ethnic groups were forced to consider themselves Turkish; and even some traditional forms of Turkish music were banned for some time. As would be expected, under the single-party dictatorship Turkey did not make economic pro-gress and society suffered decades of extreme poverty. Governing political elites took total control of the economy to curb possible opposition to their totalitarian project that aimed to recreate individuals and to remould society.

The Turkish political regime before 1950 therefore resembled the regimes the Arabs wish to escape nowadays. The Turkish people ousted the dictatorship through the ballot box and started to establish democracy. Following the Arab spring, if there are any lessons that Muslims should learn from the Turkish experiment, it is that they should follow post- rather than pre-1950 Turkey.

Conclusion

The crucial question faced by those in mainly Muslim countries in constructing an ideal political system has related to the foun-dations for such a system. Many people are eager to argue that any good system must depend on the eternal truth: *haqiqa*. Un-fortunately, although people may wish to live under the kingdom of haqiqa they differ among themselves as to what it is. Some find the haqiqa in religion, some in ethnicity, some in science and some in ideology. Wherever haqiqa lies, any and every system that relies on a single haqiqa will inevitably be oppressive. Because there are different haqiqas for different peoples, even for different individuals, to make a single haqiqa reign over others by force must bring oppression, war and bloodshed.

Therefore, what needs to be done is not to try to build up political systems that depend on this or that haqiqa, but to create a system within which the individuals and groups who subscribe to different haqiqas can live together in peace and relative harmony. Such a system has to depend on what we must call framework values, values which do not impose any specific haqiqa upon inhabitants in the country. Those values make us understand that, in order to be respected by others, we have to respect others. This inevitably requires the application of classical liberal values. Stated differently, rather than establishing a free world based on an Islamic understanding of positive freedom, a free world based on a negative understanding of freedom that accommodates different values must be established. In the words of Roskin and Coyle, in the Islamic world, nationalism, socialism and tribalism have all been tried (Roskin and Coyle 2008). The only way not tried yet is free-market liberalism. We think it is time for Muslims to discover liberal values and to look for support for them in Allah's small and big books.

References

'Abd al-Raziq, A. (1998) Message not government, religion not state. In *Liberal Islam: A Sourcebook* (ed. C. Kurzman; transl. J. Massad). Oxford University Press.

Akyol, M. (2011) *Islam without Extremes: A Muslim Case for Liberty*. New York: W. W. Norton.

Başdemir, H. Y. (2010) İslam ve Özgürlük: Negatifçi ve Pozitifçi Yaklaşımlar [Islam and liberty: positive and negative approaches]. Unpublished presentation at the meeting of Religious Freedom, Plurality, Sunnah Tradition and Islam on 30–31 January 2010, Ankara, Turkey.

Berlin, I. (1969) Two concepts of liberty. In *Four Essays on Liberty*, pp. 118–72. Oxford University Press.

Binder, L. (1988) *Islamic Liberalism: A Critique of Development Ideologies*. University of Chicago Press.

Esposito, J. L. (1998) *Islam and Politics*, 4th edn. Syracuse University Press.

Fialali-Ansary, A. (2002) The sources of enlightened Muslim thought. In *Islam and Democracy in the Middle East* (ed. L. Diamond, M. F. Plattner and D. Brumberg). Baltimore, MD: The Johns Hopkins University Press.

Koechler, H. (2004) Muslim–Christian ties in Europe: past, present, and future. Citizens International, Penang, Malaysia (http://hanskoe cler.com/koechler-monographs.htm).

Kukathas, C. (2003) *The Liberal Archipelago*. Oxford University Press.

Masmoudi, R. A. (2002) The silenced majority. In *Islam and Democracy in the Middle East* (ed. L. Diamond, M. F. Plattner and D. Brumberg). Baltimore, MD: The Johns Hopkins University Press.

Masmoudi, R. A. (2003) What is liberal Islam? The silenced majority. *Journal of Democracy* 14(2): 40–44.

Maududi, S. A. (1985) *Political Theory of Islam*. Lahore, Pakistan: Islamic Publications.

Nasr, V. (2005) The rise of 'Muslim democracy'. *Journal of Democracy* 16(2): 13–27.

Qutb, S. (1953) *Social Justice in Islam* (published as Kotb and translated from Arabic by J. B. Hardie). Washington, DC: American Council of Learned Societies.

Qutb, S. (1988) *Ma'alim fi al-Tariq*. Cairo: Dar al-Shuruq. (Quoted in Tripp 1994.)

Rokeach, M. (1960) *The Open and Closed Mind*. New York: Basic Books.

Roskin, M. G. and Coyle, J. J. (2008) *Politics of the Middle East: Cultures and Conflicts*, 2nd edn. New Jersey, NJ: Pearson Prentice Hall.

Şahin, B. (2010) *Toleration: The Liberal Virtue*. Lanham, MD: Lexington Books.

Sorman, G. (2011) Is Islam compatible with capitalism? *City Journal*, Summer.

Tripp, C. (1994) Sayyid Qutb: the political vision. In *Pioneers of Islamic Revival* (ed. A. Rahnema), pp. 154–83. London: Zed Books.

Waldron, J. (2004) Liberalism, political and comprehensive. In *Handbook of Political Theory* (ed. G. F. Gaus and C. Kukathas), pp. 88–99. London: Sage.

3 REASON VERSUS TRADITION, FREE WILL VERSUS FATE, INTERPRETATION VERSUS LITERALISM: INTELLECTUAL UNDERPINNINGS OF THE NEGATIVE OUTLOOK FOR THE MUSLIM WORLD

Mustafa Acar[1]

Introduction

The outlook for the Muslim world today is not very bright. Political unrest, civil war, economic weakness and technological backwardness are the major characteristics of many Muslim countries, if not all. Socio-economic indicators of many Muslim countries are lower than the world averages. Military power is either non-existent, or far from being a deterrent. Why is the Muslim world in such a condition?

For a complete picture one has to refer to all possible historical, economic, political, intellectual, sociological and philosophical reasons. But this picture cannot be analysed fully within the limited scope of a single chapter. This chapter argues that there are two major factors contributing to the current undesirable conditions prevailing in the Muslim world: the Mongol invasion of the Muslim world in the thirteenth century (a political-historical factor); and the prevalence of a mentality ('traditionist'

1   I thank the participants of the 3rd International Istanbul Network for Liberty (INFoL) conference in Istanbul (17–18 March 2014) for their valuable comments. My assistant, Hüsnü Bilir, also deserves thanks for providing excellent assistance in putting some pieces together. I also thank the editors of the book for their careful and critical editing to improve the text. All the remaining errors, if any, are mine.

scripturists, or Ahl al-Hadith) that is mostly characterised by fatalism, text, narration, literalism and anti-innovation. The alternative mindset ('innovationist' exegetes, or Ahl al-Ra'y) was characterised by freedom and free will, rationalism, interpretation and innovation. The battle was won by the former.

Closely related to this historical fact is a general observation that liberal democratic values such as freedom, pluralism, multiculturalism, openness, limited government and a free market are not very welcome in the Muslim world today. Many Muslim intellectuals and decision makers, as well as ordinary citizens, are either indifferent to, sceptical of, or even antagonistic towards liberal democratic values. It is reasonable to ask why this is so. What could be the historical, social and intellectual reasons for this attitude?

This chapter argues that the answer is closely related to the fact that the 'school of tradition' won the fight against the 'school of reason' back in the medieval period. The intellectual and philosophical conflict between these two major schools, together with certain geopolitical factors, has had important and destructive consequences in the Muslim world. One of the most important causes of the ongoing poor outlook and the hostile attitude of the Muslim world towards liberal values is the failure of the Innovationists-Rationalists in their battle against the Traditionists. In essence, the fight was between these two mindsets, two different perspectives, or mentalities, which could be termed *Ahl al-Ra'y* and *Ahl al-Hadith*.

Major themes of the conflict included:

- whether or not the Quran is 'created';
- whether or not the Sunna (Tradition, the sayings of the Prophet) is an alternative source of Sharia (Islamic law);
- whether or not we have 'free will' or are subject to predestination;
- whether or not reason should dominate the text and whether analogical reasoning should precede making judgments.

There are many schools as well as figures in the history of Islamic thought involved in and contributing to these discussions. Among these major schools are Mutazilite, Murcia, Wahhabiyyah, Salafiyyah and Kelamiyyah. Similarly, among the major figures who actively contributed to these discussions are Abu Hanifa, Al-Shafi, Ahmad ibn Hanbal, Al-Ash'ari, Al-Maturidi, Al-Ghazali and Ibn Rushd. More details can be found in the related section below.

Why is this discussion important? It is important because the Muslim world is at a crossroads in the post–Cold War era and in the aftermath of the global economic crisis of 2008–9. Many Muslim countries are looking for new political and economic systems to follow. As such it is important to discuss whether Islam is inherently in conflict with freedom and plurality and we have to understand firstly why the Muslim world distanced itself from liberal values. Only then can we discuss the development of a whole new path or system based on freedom, openness and democracy. Once we explore the historical roots of the liberal values in the Muslim world, then we can offer alternative economic and political systems to the policy makers and authorities.

The key to opening this path is to understand that freedom and other liberal values are not peculiar to, nor were invented solely by, the West. They are universal values. Supporters of these values are not only Western scholars: many Muslim scholars in history have invented, asserted or defended these values as well. In this regard, a revival of 'the school of *Tawhid* and justice' (Mutazilite), or 'school of reason' as opposed to tradition, would change the whole outlook in the Muslim world.

Miserable outlook of the Muslim world: poverty within abundance?

A neutral observation would characterise the situation in the Muslim world today as 'poverty within abundance'. Natural resources are plentiful and there is a young population, sometimes with good human capital. Muslim countries have good geostrategic locations. However, many things are often lacking, including internal peace, stability, technology, self-confidence, the efficient use of resources, democracy, pluralism, free markets, freedom more generally, openness and a strong civil society.

With nearly 1.5 billion people, the Muslim world constitutes 22 per cent of the world total population. Yet, the OIC's[2] share of world GDP is only 9 per cent. The OIC includes an area with 50 per cent of the world's most valuable natural resources, i.e. oil and natural gas reserves.

The Human Development Index (HDI) is a composite index measuring the level of human development or the quality of life of different countries by referring to a number of demographic, economic and social indicators. The latest HDI, as depicted in Figure 1, does not show a bright picture for the Muslim countries. There was no Muslim country in the top 10 in 2013. The best performer is Brunei, ranking only 30th. As many as 22 OIC member states (nearly 40 per cent of them) are among the lowest performers with a score below 0.5. It is interesting to note that Turkey, which has economically been one of the best performers in the world and the best performer among OECD member states over the last decade, is still 69th in the HDI, with a score of 0.759 points.

How do Muslim countries perform when it comes to economic freedom? According to the Fraser Institute's *Economic Freedom of the World* report, there are only five OIC members among 'mostly free' countries. There are 13 in the second quintile, 13 in the third quintile and 22 Muslim countries in the 'least free' category.[3] The Index of Economic Freedom published by the *Wall Street Journal* and the Heritage Foundation produces a similar result.[4]

---

2   The largest umbrella institution representing the Muslim world is the Organization of Islamic Cooperation (OIC), which consists of 57 member states located over a huge area, ranging from Central and North Africa to the Middle East, Asia Minor (Anatolia), the Balkans, the Caucasus, Central Asia and the Far East.

3   http://www.freetheworld.com/2013/EFW2013-ch1-intro.pdf (accessed 22 July 2014).

4   http://www.heritage.org/index/ranking (accessed 22 July 2014).

Figure 1   Performance of selected OIC member states in HDI and top three performers (2015)

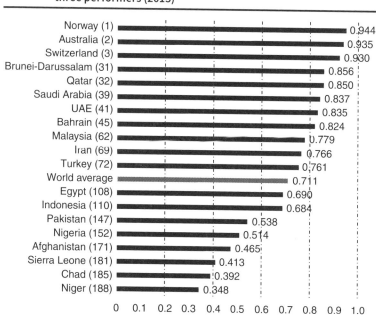

Country	HDI
Norway (1)	0.944
Australia (2)	0.935
Switzerland (3)	0.930
Brunei-Darussalam (31)	0.856
Qatar (32)	0.850
Saudi Arabia (39)	0.837
UAE (41)	0.835
Bahrain (45)	0.824
Malaysia (62)	0.779
Iran (69)	0.766
Turkey (72)	0.761
World average	0.711
Egypt (108)	0.690
Indonesia (110)	0.684
Pakistan (147)	0.538
Nigeria (152)	0.514
Afghanistan (171)	0.465
Sierra Leone (181)	0.413
Chad (185)	0.392
Niger (188)	0.348

Source: http://hdr.undp.org/en/composite/HDI (accessed 1 July 2016).

One of the critical indicators with regard to technological advancement and economic competitiveness is innovation capacity. The Global Innovation Index published by WIPO, INSEAD and Cornell University gives an indication of the innovative capacity and ability of a country to generate technology. According to the Global Innovation Index, based on 2014 data, OIC member states share the lower ranks. Malaysia is the best performer at number 33 (see Table 1).

The Global Competitiveness Index shows similar results, indicating that OIC countries are not among the dominant players in the global marketplace in terms of competitiveness. There is no Muslim country in the top ten, Qatar being the best performer in thirteenth place. The lowest performers are, once again, OIC member states.

Table 1   2014 Global Innovation Index: top 3 and selected OIC member states

Rank	Country	Score	Rank	Country	Score
1	Switzerland	64.8	47	Qatar	40.3
2	United Kingdom	62.4	54	Turkey	38.2
3	Sweden	62.3	141	Yemen	19.5
33	Malaysia	45.6	142	Togo	17.6
36	United Arab Emirates	43.2	143	Sudan	12.7
38	Saudi Arabia	41.6			

Source: http://www.globalinnovationindex.org/content.aspx?page=data-analysis

Political and intellectual reasons behind the poor performance of Muslim countries

When it comes to thinking about the reasons behind the undesirable conditions of the Muslim world today, one can think of many: political, economic, historical, intellectual-philosophical and geographical. In much of the Muslim world, there are harsh geographical, desert-like conditions with insufficient precipitation and water reserves; European colonialism was extremely damaging, as were military invasions, especially after World War I. The lack of education, military dictatorships and oppressive regimes have also retarded progress.

It is dangerous to try to conclude about causes given that we are dealing with such a complex social phenomenon. Many factors might have contributed to the unappealing conditions of Muslim geography today. However, we will focus on just two of them which, in my opinion, are relatively more important and contributed more to the end result that we see today than others: one is the Mongol invasion, which is a political-historical factor. The other is a clash of philosophies and the victory of an intellectual-philosophical position that has tended to retard progress.

The political-historical cause: the Mongol invasion

The process of large-scale invasions and destruction initiated by the famous Mongolian ruler Chingiz Khan lasted for hundreds of years from the thirteenth to the sixteenth century. There is no doubt that the Mongol (Moghul, or Mughal) invasions of the thirteenth century were one of the biggest disasters the Muslim world has ever seen. As McNeill and Waldman (1983: 248) put it:

> the Mongols, whose culture and political organization combined Chinese and nomadic pagan elements, burst upon Islam like a 'destructive storm.' By the time of Chingiz Khan's death (1227) Iran had been overrun; but the final disasters were the capture of Baghdad (1258) and the coup de grace both to the caliphate and to the irrigation that had made Iraq fertile for centuries.

The Mongol invasion resulted in economic, political and military consequences that deeply affected the fate of the Muslim world thereafter. Turkish tribes migrated from Central Asia towards the west, many of them settling down in Anatolia or Asia Minor. The Mongol invasion also played a major role in the collapse of the Muslim states in the areas today called Iran, Turkey, Iraq, Syria and the Arabian Peninsula. After the fall of Baghdad, the caliphate as a religious-political Muslim institution had to move to North Africa, and power was assumed by the Mamluks of Egypt.

On 13 February 1258, the Mongols entered Baghdad, the city of the Caliphs, then the administrative centre of the Muslim world. The Mongols showed no mercy and destroyed all the mosques, hospitals, libraries and palaces. The books from Baghdad's libraries were thrown into the Tigris River in such quantities that the river ran black with the ink from the books (Kaya 2008: 14).

We will never truly know the extent of the knowledge that was lost forever when those books were thrown into the Tigris or burned. As important as the loss of books, of course, was the loss of human life. The Mongols were known to be harsh, cruel and savage in slaughtering those who opposed them. It is estimated that between 200,000 and 1 million people were butchered in one week. Baghdad was left completely depopulated and uninhabitable. It would take centuries for Baghdad to regain any sort of prominence as an important city.[5]

After Baghdad, the Mongols continued westward. They conquered Syria from the Ayyubids, with help from the Armenians and neutrality from the Crusaders. In Palestine they reached the extent of their conquests. The new Mamluk Sultanate of Egypt, under the leadership of Baibars, defeated the Mongols at the Battle of Ain Jalut in 1260. This prevented a Mongol invasion of the Holy Lands of Mecca, Medina and Jerusalem. This also ensured the safety of the only remaining powerful Muslim empire of the time, the Mamluks.[6]

The Mongol invasion was detrimental for Muslim civilisation not only in the political and economic spheres but also in science, art, thought and philosophy. One can argue that, as a result of the Mongol invasions, the Muslim world lost everything accumulated until that time in the name of Islamic civilisation, as well as losing hundreds of thousands of men and women, including scholars, scientists and philosophers, who were murdered (Ahsan 2014: 793).

The Mongols left a deep political, economic and military scar in the heart of the Muslim world. Entire regions they invaded were depopulated. Irrigation canals, crops and economic infrastructure were destroyed beyond repair. The political institutions, such as the Caliphate, that had held the Muslim world together for centuries were simply abolished.[7]

---

5   http://lostislamichistory.com/mongols/ (accessed 23 July 2014).

6   http://lostislamichistory.com/mongols/ (accessed 23 July 2014).

7   http://lostislamichistory.com/mongols/ (accessed 23 July 2014).

The intellectual stagnation following the Mongol invasion still has its effects today. The Muslim world between the eighth and thirteenth centuries was dynamic, free and characterised by cultural, scientific and intellectual dynamism, multiculturalism, pluralism and openness. After the Mongol invasion, this bright outlook turned into a nightmare of stagnation and narrow-mindedness. Hesitance and lack of confidence were everywhere. The psychological trauma caused by this unprecedented disaster cannot be underestimated.

The intellectual-philosophical cause

The intellectual-philosophical reason behind the undesirable conditions in the Muslim world today has to do with the predominant mentality through which we look at, understand and interpret our actions. Two different schools of thought can be contrasted. One of them could be called 'innovationist', or the exegetes, and is characterised by the central importance of free will, reason, innovation, flexibility and tolerance. The opposing one, which we could describe as 'traditionist' or scripturist, is characterised by fatalism, literalism, inflexibility and intolerance. These two ways of understanding were reflected in the form of religious sects (*mazhab*), schools (Hadith versus Ra'y) or traditions. The struggle between these two different mindsets was lost by the exegetes over the course of time. Accordingly, the scripturist mentality, adopted mainly by the school of Hadith, became the dominant way of thinking in the Muslim world. This had destructive consequences that cannot be underestimated and which will be discussed below.

Main schools of thought in the Muslim world

The variety of schools of thought in the Muslim world is quite similar to that which we observe in Western thought. What comes first, text *(naql)* or reason *(aql)*? Which one is more important and which overrules the other? Narrated (oral or written) information or 'reasoned opinion' generated by our mind, intellect, brain and cognitive processes? Can human reasoning be a basis for our judgements? Can we 'interpret' the Holy Scripture, or should we take it literally? How should we understand religion and religious texts? What are the reliable sources of knowledge? How do we know the truth? Who is a good Muslim? These were hard questions and, depending on the answers given to these questions, the four major Islamic schools of thought can be categorised (Uludag 2012).

Salafiyyah (dogmatism)

According to the Salafi school or the *Salafiyyah*, 'naql' (a belief in text, tradition, narration and transmitted information) precedes 'aql' (reason, intellect, rational opinion and judgement). Narrated knowledge or text takes priority over knowledge based on logic and reason. If there is a contradiction between reason and text, reason should always be subject to the text. A literal meaning of a word should be taken as a baseline; no *te'vil* (interpretation) is permissible. For instance, Quranic expressions such as 'God sat on *Arsh*' (Divine Throne) (Quran 10:3) and 'God's hand is above their hands' (Quran 48:10) should be taken literally with no interpretation whatsoever. Any type of innovative attitude, especially in religious affairs, is regarded as a sin and blindly rejected. Every innovation is regarded as a heresy. The Salafi mentality, in short, is characterised by inflexibility and anti-pluralism: there is only one truth (*haqiqa*) and this is the truth of the Holy Scripture and the Traditions (Hadith) of the Prophet. Human interpretations are wrong and should be discarded.

This school and the mentality it adopted are clearly still alive today and serve as the source of inspiration and motivation for many radical Islamic movements throughout the Muslim world. Even though there are many minor differences between them, Islamic movements such as the Taliban, Saudi-rooted Wahhabism, ISIS (Islamic State of Iraq and Syria) and al-Qaida are all Salafi movements.

Kelamiyyah (rationalism)

Kelam can be defined as the discipline or theological-religious philosophy of investigating Islamic beliefs and religious-philosophical theories and aiming at explaining or proving faith-related issues with rational proofs. The main concern of the Kelamiyyah school was to defend Islam on the basis of reason and rational arguments. According to Kelam, any valid argument should be based on logic and reason. If there is a contradiction between reason and the text, reason should take priority. Te'vil (interpretation) of the religious text is allowed and should be encouraged. Reasoned opinion or one's own ideas (Ra'y) should be used to generate knowledge and judgement should be applied when there is not an open, simple, direct Quranic verse to resolve a problem.

There is no distinct Kelami movement in the Muslim world today. Many discussions of the Kelamiyyah of the early periods are no longer as active today as they used to be. Major historical figures of Kelam include al-Ash'ari (d. 935), al-Maturidi[8] (d. 945), Wasil ibn Atâ (d. 748), Cuveyni (d. 1085), Allâf (d. 850), Ibrahim ibn Sayyar al-Nazzam (d. 846), Amr ibn Bahr al-Jahiz (d. 869), Zemahsheri (d. 1144), Taftazâni (d. 1390) and Cürcâni (d. 1413).

Sufiyyah (mysticism)

Intuition, inspiration, self-discovery and an internal spiritual journey are the key words for the Sufi school. According to Sufiyyah, reason and text are not that important and both should be subject to intuition. What is important is intuitive knowledge or what your 'heart' tells you. Literalism is rejected by the Sufiyyah school. Moral purification is regarded as extremely important. People may follow an abstract, subjective,

---

8   See Düzgün (2011) for a detailed discussion on al-Maturidi and his contribution to Islamic thought.

spiritual journey through music, dreams and intuition and this is regarded as more important than intellectual, philosophical or rational discussion.

The school of Sufiyyah, of Islamic mysticism, is still alive today and in conflict with the Salafi school. Salafiyyah condemns Sufiyyah as following a way that combines un-Islamic beliefs, fairy tales and superstition. This school is the most interesting and attractive among alternative Islamic movements in the eyes of Westerners and non-Muslims.

Felasifah (philosophy)

The school of philosophy is based on unguided, pure reason. Pioneers and founding fathers of *felasifah* were inspired by the great ancient Greek philosophers such as Aristotle, Socrates and Plato. According to this school of thought, pure reason could discover the truth even if there were no revelation, no prophets or no other guide. Reason, intellect, syllogism and intellectual endeavour are at the centre of understanding reality and of creating knowledge.

All the discussions, debates and fights on the nature of truth, reality and the true path have taken place within these four major schools of thought in Muslim history. For the sake of our discussion, the relatively more important arguments with regard to shaping the mentality of later generations were centred around reason versus tradition, free will versus fate and interpretation versus literalism, which we will discuss below.

Reason versus tradition, Ra'y versus Hadith, free will versus fate, interpretation versus literalism

The emergence of the four major schools of thought discussed above was not of course instant; it took hundreds of years. On the way, political disputes and power struggles played a significant role in shaping these theoretical-intellectual discussions.

The first major dispute and break-up in Muslim society erupted during the reign of the fourth Caliph, Ali, who was cousin and son-in-law of the Prophet Muhammad (pbuh).[9] The ostensible source of the conflict was the desire to punish the assassins of the third Caliph, Othman. But the real reason was the power struggle over who was going to be the next ruler. Eventually, a war erupted between the supporters of Ali and Muawiyah (the then Governor of Damascus). A third group called *Kharijiyyah* (outers, or outsiders, belonging to no side) then emerged which argued that both sides were wrong and that neither Ali nor Muawiyah should be recognised as the Caliph; both sides should be called to repent and if they did not, they should be killed.

In the following years a number of ideological and religious disputes emerged out of this originally political conflict. Indeed, many of the intellectual, theoretical, philosophical, ideological and religious disputes in Muslim history have political roots, directly or indirectly. Over the course of time, political unrest and reaction intermingled and turned into intellectual, philosophical, ideological and religious disputes.

As far as the issues of freedom, free will, fate or predestination and the interpretation of the Holy Scripture are concerned, one can argue that the aforementioned four major schools or lines of thought can ultimately be consolidated into two types of mindset, summarised below.

School of free will

The discussion on 'free will versus fate' started very early in Islamic history. The founding father of the school of free will is Muhammad ibn Hanafiyyah, son of Ali, the fourth Caliph. Among the main figures of this school are Amr al-Maqsus, Ma'bad

---

9   Pbuh: Peace be upon him, an expression Muslims use when the name of the Prophet is mentioned.

al-Juhani, Gaylan al-Dimeshkî, al-Ja'd bin Dirham, Hasan al-Basri and Jahm bin Safwan. The main argument of this school is that the human will is free. There is no such thing as preordained destiny. Human beings prepare their own destiny as they are in charge of their own actions. The same line of argument would be adopted later by the school of Tawhid and justice, more widely known as the Mutazilites.

The historical roots of this school are political, economic and ideological and they also emanate from resistance to the oppression by the Umayyad regime (660–750). The basic sources of unrest were the oppressive treatment of the Sultanate, Arab nationalism, social injustice, income inequality and humiliation of non-Arabs. This unrest triggered antagonistic and opposing ideas. The fact that the Umayyad Dynasty legitimised their oppressive actions 'in the name of God' or 'by God's command' prompted the reaction of the school of free will.

School of Tawhid and justice: Mutazilite

The school of Tawhid and justice, more commonly known as the Mutazilite school, is no doubt the most rationalist and pro-free-will school in Islamic history. The main figures include Wasil ibn Atâ (d. 748), Amr ibn Ubayd (d. 761), Abu al-Hudhail al-Allaf (d. 840), Ibrahim ibn Sayyar al-Nazzam (d. 846), Mu'ammar ibn Khayyat Abbad (d. 842), Bishr ibn al-Mu'tamir (d. 825), Amr ibn Bahr al-Jahiz (d. 869), abu Ali al-Jubbai (d. 849), Qadi 'Abd al-Jabbar (d. 1023), Zemahşeri (d. 1144) and al-Maturidi (d. 945). All these scholars are also among the major figures of the *Kelamiyyah* school and tried to understand, explain and defend Islamic beliefs and commands on the basis of *aql* (reason), logic and rational argumentation. Eliacik describes this school as 'the main thinking dynamics' of the history of Islamic thought, because a huge collection of *kelam* (theological philosophy), *fiqh* (jurisprudence), politics and *tafsir* (interpretation of the Quran) have been centred around the ideas put forward by the Mutalizites.

Heavily criticised by some conservative, fatalist schools, the Mutazilite school argued that Allah (God) is the *Alim* (all-knower, wise, omniscient) and *Adil* (just). Hence wrongdoing, oppression and cruelty cannot be ascribed to Him because He commands human beings to be just and to keep away from oppression: it is not logical for Him to act otherwise. Therefore, choices between good and evil, belief and disbelief, obedience and disobedience, all these are actions that belong to human beings. Hence, it is human beings who choose or determine their own actions; there is no such thing as predetermined destiny. Responsibility requires free will, and that requires human beings to make choices. Ibn Hazm and Wasil ibn Atâ argued that: 'If we hold the view that human beings are acting according to a pre-determined fate, then the whole foundations of morality and religious law would collapse' (Eliacik 2001: 200).

Another argument with important religious-philosophical implications raised by the Mutazilites was the 'createdness of the Quran'. The Mutazilites adopted the view that the Quran is created. That is, it existed at a certain point in time and was not eternal. Only God's 'being' is eternal; everything else is created later in time.

Mutazilites also argue in favour of the existence of *al-manzilah bain al-manzilatain* (a middle ground between two stops): there will be a middle ground for those who committed great sins; this ground will be neither Hell, nor Paradise. This argument originally arose out of the discussion over who was right and who was wrong in the clash between Ali and Muawiyah – who is going to go to Paradise and who to Hell? The school of Murcie (the 'Postponers') argued that we cannot know for sure who was right, only God knows this. So, instead of disputing and fighting over an issue we can never solve, it is better to 'postpone' it to the hereafter. Mutazilites adopted this view that, although one side of the dispute must be right and the other wrong, we cannot be sure who is right and wrong until the hereafter.

The crucial importance of this argument lies in its link with the idea of pluralism. Once you accept the idea that something goes beyond the limits of our knowledge, we cannot know the answer for sure and we do not have to take a side on the issue. Then we are ready to accept that both sides might be right within certain limits or that we will never be able to resolve who is right during our time on earth; hence the idea of pluralism.[10]

School of reason: Ahl al-Ra'y

Closely related to the school of Mutazilites is the school of Ra'y or 'Ahl al-Ra'y' as it is known in the Islamic literature. This is a school that has followed a rationalist line of thought. One can argue that the Mutazilites and Ahl al-Ra'y are twin sisters in that the former are the rationalists of religious-theological philosophy and the latter are rationalists in the area of jurisprudence.

The following are some of the arguments adopted by or inspired by the pioneers of this school (Eliacik 2001: 167–68):

- I use my *aql* (reason) to make *ijtihad* (make judgements).
- This is in contradiction with the Quran.
- If the Prophet was alive, He would go this way.
- Times have changed.
- Those conditions are no longer valid.
- The purpose of the Prophet/Quran was such and such.
- Literal meaning is not what we look at.
- Since the cause is the same, the judgement should also be the same ('qıyas', syllogism).
- The common good requires this ('maslahat al-murselah').
- This is more useful ('celb al-menafi').
- Doing this is more logical and rational ('*istihsan*').

---

10 A thorough discussion on the Mutazilite school can be found in Ammara (1998). Cabiri (1997a) is also a good source about Muslim–Arab thinking in the formation period.

- Since it is not explicitly forbidden, then it must be permissible ('*istihsab*').
- This Hadith (religious tradition, or the sayings of the Prophet) is in contradiction with the Quran (critique of the text).
- The narrator is not a reliable one (critique of Hadith).
- This is against the customary practice.

Ahl al-Ra'y argued that reason, or 'reasoned opinion' (Ra'y), is an important source of judgement, more reliable than the weak Hadith (tradition, or alleged sayings of the Prophet). The weak or unsound Hadith should not be used as a basis for judgement. This school, especially the founding father Abu Hanifa, was very creative in inventing new tools to find solutions to the daily problems Muslims encountered in their social and commercial life. According to this school, after the Quran and Sunna (sound Hadith), the following can also be used for generating judgement: qıyas (syllogism); istishan; istishab; the common good; and customs and traditions of the society. It was Abu Hanifa who judged that an adult and mature woman can get married without the consent of her parents; that the Quran can be translated into another language; and that the Quran is created.

School of tradition: Ahl al-Hadith

This school represents a traditionist mentality which is literalist, fatalist, conservative and anti-innovationist. It was completely opposed to the 'innovationist' mentality represented by Ahl al-Ra'y. The founding fathers of three of the four major schools of jurisprudence in Islam are among the main figures of Ahl al-Hadith: Ahmad ibn Hanbal, Imam Malik and Imam al-Shafi'i.

The arguments put forward by the scholars of Ahl al-Ra'y led to a reaction from the scholars of Ahl al-Hadith. They criticised the rational-logical arguments of Ahl al-Ra'y as 'they mix their reason with the religion; he makes judgement according to his wish or pleasure; he is bringing *bid'ah* (innovation) into the religion; was there such a thing during the Prophet, no; this is against Quran and Sunna (religious tradition); he rejects Hadith because it does not suit his purpose; he is making new inventions'. When Umar ibn al-Khattab suggested the compilation of the Quranic verses in a book two years after the death of the Prophet, the idea was rejected and he was criticised on the grounds that the Prophet himself did not try such a thing (Eliacik 2001: 168). In other words, the clash between innovationists and traditionists (liberal versus conservative in a sense), between those who were for and those who were against change and innovation, had started as early as the death of the Prophet.

The main arguments of this school include the following:

- Hadiths, the sayings of the Prophet (pbuh) are as important and authoritative as the Quran.
- Reason, personal opinion or individual ideas should not be taken as a source of judgement.
- 'Of all things, the worst is innovation in religion. Every new thing in religion is an innovation (bid'ah); every innovation is a deviation; every deviation leads to Hellfire'.[11]

All the above disputes and schools can be reduced to two: Ahl al-Ra'y versus Ahl al-Hadith, or reason versus tradition. The fight was lost by the former, affecting deeply the later destiny of the intellectual as well as socio-political journey of the Muslim world.

---

11 A good account and fruitful discussion on 'Sunna vs reason' or 'Ra'y vs Hadith' can be found in Akyol (2011), especially chapters 3 and 4 on the medieval war of ideas (pp. 80–116). See also Kocyigit (1988) for a detailed discussion on the debates between scholars of Hadith and Kalam.

Intellectual conflicts with political roots and implications

There were many areas of debate among Islamic scholars. Almost all of these debates either originated from particular political conflicts or had specific political implications. We will examine three of these debates: *qadar* (fate) versus free will; whether faith be subject to increase or decrease; and whether the Quran is created or not.

Fate versus free will

One group called Jabriyyah (fatalists) argued that all we do and all we experience is imposed upon us by God. In other words, our fate is preordained and prewritten, so that there is no way to escape from it. The other group called Qadariyyah (supporters of free will) argued that there is no preordained, inescapable fate: human beings can determine their actions by their own free will. Some extreme versions of this line of thought (Mu'tazilah) argued that 'men create their own actions'. As Ma'bad al-Juhani put it, there is no preordained destiny; events can be known as they happen (Eliacik 2001: 125).

There are two important implications of this debate. The first one is about responsibility. Who is responsible for what is happening? Men, or God? We, or the Creator? If God determines everything before it happens and dictates it, then we cannot be responsible for our deeds since 'it is our fate, written on our foreheads'. On the other hand, if men can determine their own actions, then they are responsible for them.

The second implication is a political one. The Umayyad Dynasty liked the argument for fate, using it as a justification for their oppressive rule. They argued that what was happening was 'our fate' ordained by God. If God had not wanted all that was happening, He would not have allowed it to happen at all. So, people were expected to take oppressive rule as a preordained fate and obey. In fact this fatalist view and attitude was adopted and became so widespread in Muslim societies that authoritative, oppressive dictatorships and dynasties throughout the Muslim world made use of it to legitimise their wrongdoings.

Can faith ('iman') be subject to increase and decrease?

One line of thought argued that 'there is no increase or decrease in faith' (i.e. *iman*: belief in God and the Day of Judgement). Faith either exists or does not exist; it does not increase or decrease. A man can be either a believer ('*Mu'min*') or an unbeliever ('*Qafir*'); one cannot talk about someone as a 'half believer'. On the other hand, some believed the opposite – that faith can increase or decrease, hence somebody may be a 'full believer' or 'half believer.'

An interesting political implication of the second line of argument was closely related to the taxation of newly converted Muslim tribes. According to Islamic jurisprudence at the time, Muslims did not have to pay taxes (they paid *zakat*, religious charity); but non-Muslim minorities living in the society did have to pay taxes in exchange for the security provided by the Muslim authority. When political authority accepted the line of thought that faith can 'increase' or 'decrease', it then became possible to tax the new converts because their faith was not 'strong enough' yet. This is another example where a seemingly intellectual-ideological-religious debate is closely related to political disputes.

Is the Quran 'created'?

One line of thought argued that the 'Quran is not created': it was eternal and had existed with God since before the beginning of time. Others argued that the Quran was created: it was not eternal but created by God at a particular point in time. This debate also has very important implications.

Once the idea of an 'uncreated, eternal Quran' is adopted, it immediately becomes 'untouchable' and not open to interpretation (te'vil) by human persons: it is eternal and has existed with God since the eternal beginning. Therefore, every single word of the Quran should also be eternal, not open to debate, dispute, rereading or reinterpretation in a particular historical-social context. As would be expected, a strong literalism, word-by-word translation and accepting of the ambiguous verses of the Quran 'as is' (*bi-la kaif*; i.e. without asking 'how?') followed from this way of thinking.

On the other hand, if the idea of a 'created' Quran is adopted, then it becomes permissible to reread and reinterpret it in a particular context. This way of thinking was more open to pluralism and a variety of different meanings and interpretations of the same original text.

Abu Hanifa and his followers (Ahl al-Ra'y) believed that the Quran was created, whereas ibn Hanbal and his followers (Ahl al-Hadith) were strongly against this idea, believing that the Quran was uncreated, and hence not open to interpretation.

One can, once again, easily see the connection between this debate and the ongoing debates about change versus status quo, liberalism versus conservatism, monotype versus pluralism and open-mindedness versus narrow-mindedness.

Social-cultural base of the confrontation: Arabs versus non-Arabs

It is interesting to note that the vast majority of the pioneers of the traditionists (Ahl al-Hadith) had the following characteristics: they were of Arab origin; they belonged to aristocratic families; engaged more in rural and agrarian affairs; they were supported mostly by nomads; and they focused more on agriculture than other economic activities. On the other hand, the majority of the pioneers of the Rationalists or Innovationists (Ahl al-Ra'y) had the following social and cultural characteristics: they were non-Arab ('Mawali', immigrants, captives, slaves, Persian or Central Asian), lived in more developed urban areas and engaged in non-agricultural, non-rural activities such as trade, commerce and urban artisanships. For instance, the most prominent figure of the rationalist Mutazilite school, Vasıl b. Ata (d. 748), was the son of a slave from a non-Arab family. Likewise, the leading figure of the Ahl al-Ra'y school, Abu Hanifah (d. 767), was born and raised in Kufa (Iraq); his grandfather was a slave taken captive during the conquest of Iran and was freed later on. His ancestors had migrated from Kabul (Afghanistan) to Kufa (Eliacik 2001: 179, 198).

The great Muslim philosopher Ibn Khaldun (2013) argued that geography, climatic conditions and the subsistence way of living have a determining power on one's lifestyle and way of thinking. Obviously, these conditions are not the same in rural and urban areas. The rural areas are characterised by harsh natural conditions and a nomadic or agrarian way of living. Life in rural areas is relatively simple. Living conditions are more basic, with no or few public services and less variety of possibilities to make a livelihood. On the other hand, urban areas are characterised by a settled, complicated life with greater sophistication and more possibilities for commercial and industrial activities, artisanship, the provision of services and different opportunities for earning money and making a living. Ibn Khaldun seems to be right when we link the followers of each line of thought and the environmental-cultural conditions.

The school of reason eventually lost the fight and the school of Hadith won. There are various reasons proposed as an explanation for the decline of the rationalist school and the triumph of the traditionist school. To some, the rationalist school was an alien import from ancient Greece that was 'incompatible with a Quranic worldview' (Robinson 1996: 92). For some others, influential Muslim figures such as Imam Gazali (d. 1111) were responsible for this decline. However, in the author's opinion,

Akyol is right when he says 'it was not the Quranic worldview but the post-Quranic tradition that overshadowed Islamic reason. The political authorities (Umayyad and Abbasid Caliphs) of the time played a major role in the course of this confrontation by supporting the traditionists most of the time' (Akyol 2011: 117–118).

Conclusion: destructive consequences of the conflict between reason and tradition

The fact that the conflict between the school of reason and the school of tradition ended in favour of the latter had destructive consequences. The most important negative consequence is reflected in the sceptical, hesitant or even hostile attitude of Muslim societies to such liberal values as freedom, plurality, civil society, democracy, free markets and innovation. However, it should be stressed that the hostility or scepticism towards these values is not intrinsic to Islam. In other words, it is a matter of the mentality and perspective through which one reads, understands and interprets the main sources of Islam, specifically the Quran and the Sunna. In fact, there has been an alternative line of thinking since the early ages of Islam which is pro-freedom, pro-plurality and pro-free-market.

The traditionist school won the dispute and their arguments were adopted or supported by the then political authorities. Philosophy and reason and the idea of plurality lost their reputation in society. The weak or unsound Hadith were taken as guides in political life rather than reasoned opinion, logic and analogy. Fatalist views – believing that everything happens according to a prewritten destiny – were adopted by the majority of the Muslim Umma. Even the followers of the rationalist Hanafite school became adherents or passive followers of traditionists. This explains, to a great extent, why the Muslim world is hesitant or sceptical about liberal values.

Obviously, it is not possible to reverse the course of history. But we can do something, as responsible intellectuals, to shape the future so as to create a more open, free, productive and prosperous Muslim world. What we need to do, as Muslim intellectuals, is to go back to the history of Islamic thought, reread and rethink the debates and discussions on free will, destiny, createdness (and hence the permissibility of interpretation) of the Holy Scripture, freedom of thought, plurality and free markets,[12] and translate it into today's language. Fortunately, this is happening. Muslim intellectuals have started to argue that anticapitalist attitudes are not consistent with Islam's historical experience and Islam's theological attitude towards economic activity and the pursuit of profit. In fact Islam, which was conveyed by a businessman (Prophet Muhammad was a successful trader in most of his life) and has held commercial activities in high regard since its beginning, is quite in harmony with a capitalist system strengthened by moral values with regard to helping the poor and needy (Çizakça and Akyol 2012: 14).

A revival of the innovationist, pro-freedom, rationalist school at the intellectual and philosophical levels will help pave the way to an open, civil and free society in the Muslim world. This will help create a social and political transformation in Muslim societies.

References

Acar, M. and Akin, B. (2013) Islam and market economy: friend or foe? Paper presented to the 2nd International INFoL Conference, Islamabad, Pakistan, 1–2 March 2013.

Ahsan, A. S. (2014) Fall of the Abbasid Caliphate. In *A History of Muslim Philosophy* (ed. M. M. Sharif), Volume 2, Book Four, pp. 789–95.

---

12 More can be found on Islam and the free-market economy in Acar and Akin (2013).

Pakistan Philosophical Congress. http://www.muslimphilosophy. com/hmp/XL-Fourty.pdf. (Originally published in 1963, Wiesbaden: Otto Harrassowitz.)

Akkuş, M. (2012) Ermenilerin İlhanlı Dini Siyasetindeki Rolleri [The role of Armenians in the religious politics of Ilkhanids]. *Türkiyat Araştırmaları Dergisi* 31: 205–21.

Akyol, M. (2011) *Islam without Extremes: A Muslim Case for Liberty.* W. W. Norton. (Translation from the Turkish: *Özgürlüğün İslami Yolu,* Translated by Ömer Baldık. Istanbul: Doğan Kitap, 2013.)

Ammara, M. (1998) *t ve İnsanın Özgürlüğü Sorunu* [Mu'tazilite and the problem of human freedom] (translated by V. Ince). Istanbul: Ekin Yayınları.

Cabiri, M. A. (1997a) *Arap–İslam Aklının Oluşumu* [*The Formation of the Arab–Islamic Mind*] (translated by İ. Akbaba). İstanbul: Kitabevi Pub.

Cabiri, M. A. (1997b) *İslam'da Siyasal Akıl* [*Political Mind in Islam*] (translated by V. Akyüz). İstanbul: Kitabevi Publications.

Cizakca, M. and Akyol, M. (2012) *Ahlaki Kapitalizm* [*Moral Capitalism*]. Istanbul: Ufuk Publications.

Düzgün, S. A. (ed.) (2011) *Mâturîdî'nin Düşünce Dünyası* [*The Realm of Thought of Maturidi*]. Ankara: Ministry of Culture and Tourism.

Eliacik, R. İ. (2001) *İslâm'ın Yenilikçileri: İslâm Düşünce Tarihinde Yenilik Arayışları* [*Islam's Innovationists: Pursuit of Innovation in the History of Islamic Thought*], 3rd edn, Volume I. Istanbul: Medcezir Pub.

Global Competitiveness Index: http://www3.weforum.org/docs/GCR20 13-14/GCR_Rankings_2013-14.pdf (accessed 22 July 2014).

Global Innovation Index: http://www.globalinnovationindex.org/cont ent.aspx?page=data-analysis (accessed 22 July 2014).

Global Firepower Data: http://www.globalfirepower.com/ (accessed 14 August 2014).

Ibn Khaldun (2013) *Mukaddime* [*Muqaddimah*] (translated by S. Uludağ). Istanbul: Dergah.

Kaya, S. (2008) Büyük Selçuklular Döneminde Bağdat. *Akademik Bakış* 15: 1–16.

Kocyigit, T. (1988) *Hadisçilerle Kelamcılar Arasındaki Münakaşalar* [*Debates Between Scholars of Hadith and Kalam*], 3rd edn. Ankara: T. Diyanet Vakfı Yayınları.

McNeill, W. H. and Waldman, M. R. (eds) (1983) *The Islamic World*. University of Chicago Press.

Robinson, F. (ed.) (1996) *The Cambridge Illustrated History of the Islamic World*. Cambridge University Press.

Stockholm International Peace Research Institute: http://www.sipri.org/yearbook/2013/03 (accessed 22 July 2014).

Uludag, S. (2012) *İslam Düsüncesinin Yapısı* [*The Structure of Islamic Thought*], 7th edn. Istanbul: Dergah Publications.

UNDP (United Nations Development Program): https://data.undp.org/dataset/Table-3-Inequality-adjusted-Human-Development-Inde/9jnv-7hyp (accessed 22 July 2014).

4 WELFARE BEYOND THE STATE: 'IHSANI' SOCIETAL-BASED WELFARE

Maszlee Malik

Introduction

The Islamic world view regards the human person as created to be the vice-regent (Caliph) of God on earth with a mission to be pursued. This world view shapes the aspiration and vision of Muslims and helps turn people into 'functioning individuals' who dedicate themselves to this duty in order to attain *falah* (holistic success in this world and the next) (see Quran 2:189, 3:130, 3:200, 5:35, 5:100, 24:31, 28:67 and 24:51).

This does not lead to the creation of an imaginary, utopian society based purely on theory without consideration for reality. To achieve their goals, individuals will actively be working to promote society's 'well-being' and the creation of 'social capital', or *ihsani* capital. Indeed, these things are currently accepted by many people who are not Muslim as an effective aspect of the promotion of economic development, equality, participation and democracy. Increasing evidence shows that social cohesion is critical for societies to prosper economically and for development to be sustainable (World Bank 1999).

Material objectives are not the ultimate aims of the Islamic-motivated struggle for development. The achievement of material enrichment emerges as a result of individuals exercising their 'inner' conviction to attain falah through the culture of ihsan (perfection).[1] Those individuals are not living individually in the pursuit only of their own aims, but rather acting collectively with a spirit of solidarity and sharing their ideals with others. The struggle of the functioning individual to pursue his own well-being and that of the community not only manifests itself in the ritual-spirituality of the individual, but also represents the true meaning of striving in the way of Allah (jihad). Jihad in its broader meaning encompasses the struggle for individual development, justice, humanity and well-being (Taleqani 1986: 54–56).

Functioning individuals and ihsani social capital

Individuals, however, cannot function in a vacuum within a minimal state. To bring the Muslim *Umma* (community) to perfection requires the establishment of a benevolent society comprising functioning individuals. With the spirit of universal solidarity among its individuals, the benevolent society will maximise the potential of its members to be independent, to flourish and to bring about their falah.

Individuals are able to function properly and flourish within a benevolent society which comprises families and groups of individuals mutually or collectively sharing their passion to achieve shared goals. By the same token, the benevolent society is brought about as the result of the interrelated networking of the functioning individuals. The Quran states that the functioning individual's mission is the continuation of the Prophet Muhammad's mission as the agent of mercy to the universe. This is evidenced in the following verse of the Quran: 'For I [Allah] have created you [Muhammad] to be nothing but a blessing for all creation' (Quran 21:107).

---

1   *Ihsan* (perfection) means the comprehensive excellence, and the final crowning glory or finishing embellishment. It incorporates beneficence, performance of good conduct and acts of mercy (Ibn Manzur 1956; 13:117; Wehr 1979: 209) including spending wealth for the welfare of humankind (2:195, 3:134), being kind to the parents (46:15), being generous (2:236), paying *zakat* (charity or alms) (31:3, 11:114–15) (Malik 2014).

The benevolent society will lead to the creation of a 'virtuous society' that will articulate the Islamic-inspired way to bring development and the eradication of poverty within the larger sphere of economically functioning individuals. The next section will elaborate further on how the benevolent society, as an element of ihsani, is essential in constructing the big picture of societal-based welfare discussed in this chapter.

A benevolent society as an alternative to the state as provider

As mentioned above, functioning individuals do not work in a vacuum. Individuals operate within a society that enables them to be fully functioning. A 'big society' in which individuals are politically and economically less dependent on the state but are interdependent on each other is necessary to create a virtuous society.

This paradigm does not deny the importance of individualism but recognises that individuals are interdependent and do not only pursue their personal interests. Individuals collectively assist each other by pursuing their own personal falah, but also help each other in reaching theirs. This requires that horizontal relationships across society are governed by justice, benevolence and mercy. Such an Islamic-inspired society could best be described as a 'benevolent society'.

By the same token, this benevolent society itself is the result of the intercommunicating and interrelated networking of the functioning individuals within the culture of ihsan, which demands that every single individual not only achieves his personal well-being by creating a falah of his own, but also cultivates an environment which can facilitate the falah for others. This collective mutually interdependent nature of functioning individuals is the gist of the *Tawhidi* reality (Malik 2011: 269).

The Tawhidi principle leads to the realisation of *amanah* (trust) by preserving individual rights while also enabling individuals to execute their obligations in a just and benevolent manner. It is stated in the Quran (4:58): 'Allah commands you to deliver the trusts to those to whom they are due; and whenever you judge between people, judge with justice...' Thus, the principles of justice and benevolence require individuals to live and pursue their lives not only for their own personal interest, but also as agents of mercy to mankind through the spirit of *ukhuwwah* (brotherhood).

This can be clearly understood from various verses of the Quran and the Prophetic tradition, which explain certain values or qualities of sharing and caring to be adopted by Muslims during their lives. For example, it was stated (Quran 5:2): 'And cooperate with one another in all that is good and pious and do not cooperate in sin and aggression'. In chapter 59 (al-Hasyr), verse nine, it was recorded that Allah praises the *Ansar* (Muslim community in Medina) during *Hijrah* (migration of Prophet Muhammad and his companions to Medina from Mecca) due to the altruistic spirit shown by their sacrifices for the welfare of the *Muhajirin* (people of Mecca). An important landmark example of the pivotal role of unity in Islamic tradition was the establishment of brotherhood between the Ansar and Muhajirin: 'But those who before them, had homes (in Medina) and had adopted the faith, show their affection to such as came to them for refuge, and entertain no desire in their hearts for things given to the (latter), but give them preference over themselves, even though poverty was their (own lot). And those saved from the covetousness of their own souls, they are the ones that achieve prosperity' (Quran 59:9).

When the Muhajirin were compelled to migrate to Yathrib (thenceforth known as Medina) due to persecution in Mecca, they were immediately reconciled to the people of Medina on the basis of what was then a unique concept of ukhuwwah (fraternity). In an unprecedented act of magnanimity, the Medina Muslims (who came to be collectively known as the Ansar or helpers) agreed to share their wealth and property with the Muhajirin.

The Ansar gave a portion of their homes to the Muhajirin families for their use, and allowed them to farm on their lands under a system of sharecropping.

A benevolent society that mutually connects individuals and brings them to a state of social cohesion leads to 'social capital' through the empowerment of each of society's members (Malik 2011: 269). Social capital in the context of the benevolent society would promote the well-being of the community. At the societal level, it will lead to the maximisation of economic well-being of individuals along with the promotion of social well-being.

This process has to be built on the institution of the family. Islamic moral teachings emphasise the value of the family. Without the institution of the family that enables individuals to function, and Islamic values to prevail, it is hard to create the benevolent society. Strong family institutions with Islamic values will ensure social networking among society members to establish the ihsani social capital. The effective role of families and social networking under the influence of culture, virtue and religious values is acknowledged by many researchers of development and social capital as another factor that promotes holistic and comprehensive development (Chang 1997; Newton 1997; Kliksberg 2001).

Universal solidarity within this benevolent society expands beyond issues of political economy and a discourse based on principles of ownership and rights. The benevolent society presupposes the crucial elements of family, socialisation, education, a strong ethos, ritual-spiritual practice and the exercise of moral values and personal responsibility. It is through this process that virtues and values are kept alive in the lives of individuals and families. However, it should be noted that such expressions of solidarity do not imply by any means a socialistic approach. Instead, we should focus on the development of individual lives by promoting the right microdynamics of society. This also fits into the new development paradigm, which has shifted the focus from macroeconomic development to microdynamics.

Ihsani, social capital, can only be achieved within the framework of an effective minimal state where there is more room for the society's dynamism to be fully exercised through state and non-state institutions. Social capital requires opportunities for people to flourish without the hindrance and interference of the state. If a state is to encourage a benevolent society to flourish, it should allow non-state institutions through which individuals and society can be actively involved in promoting the development of social capital. The necessary interdependency between the state and society (represented by individuals and groups that develop spontaneously) is exemplified through effective civil society institutions. Correspondingly, within this framework, participants in civil society will be able to assume responsibility for social and economic development including the provision of essential services in education and public health.

The Islamic notion of civil society emerges from the inner foundation of the functioning individual. Keane asserts that the emergence of civil society could be traced in Islamic history through the flourishing of social institutions in Muslim societies in the past (Keane 2009: 133–36). The civil society (*al-mujtama' al-madani*) that emerged was mainly motivated by economic factors that promoted ownership and provided welfare. The *waqf* was identified as a civil society institution developed by early Muslim societies that enabled people to resist vigorously any attempts by the state to take over the wealth of individuals.

The dynamo of civil society is not personal interest or the mere protection of individual rights against the state, but it was part of the articulation of the individuals' conviction in achieving *falah* through the culture of ihsan (Malik 2014). In sum, civil society under the *Tawhidi* paradigm reflects the degree of religiosity of individuals in maintaining their vertical relationship with God and their horizontal relationship with their fellow human persons as well as with the environment.

Welfare through waqfs

From the earliest days, Islamic societies have developed various institutions for the fulfilment of the basic needs of all in society (Zarqa 1988). The institutions include, among others, *zakat* (the provision of charity or alms) and *waqf* (land, property or cash used for charitable purposes).

A waqf is the most important institution for enshrining the Islamic ethos, balancing private ownership and communal obligations. The fundamental idea of waqf was to bring the profound ideal of philanthropic and benevolent attitudes within society into reality. The waqf is not unlike the English trust. The originator places property or money into the waqf and the endowment is then used for the stated charitable purposes. They have existed since the earliest Islamic times. The intention is that the waqf can last forever, but in reality they can be wound up under certain circumstances. When the waqf is created, the founder states the purpose and potential beneficiaries (for example, poor members of the family, migrants or the whole community). Non-Muslims can be beneficiaries, but not if they are in conflict with Muslims.

Since the dawn of the practice, the idea of the waqf was very inclusive and expanded beyond religious to social and welfare purposes. The Prophet Muhammad encouraged his companions to use waqf for both religious and worldly purposes. The establishment of mosques for worship and community activities, building wells for the use of the early Muslim community in Medina, horses for use in war and lands cultivated for feeding the poor were all financed by waqfs by early Muslims under the supervision and guidance of the Prophet Muhammad himself. The practice continued and was later expanded by the following Muslim generations. The waqf continued to become the heartbeat of the Muslim community and survived in both its religious and worldly forms (Gil 1998).

The waqf formed a concrete foundation for wealthy individuals in society to share their wealth with the unfortunate as part of their social contribution, without any element of intervention or enforcement by the state. Keane (2009: 136–38) implies that the waqf was among the earliest vehicles to have represented civil society since the dawn of Muslim history. The waqf, along with zakat (alms), has contributed towards the economic well-being of Muslim societies for centuries by creating a space for the development of a societal-based welfare system (Lewis 1990: 38–41; Hoexter 1998; Baskan 2002). The waqf enabled individuals and society to be independent from the state. The waqf system contributed to the flourishing of mosques, orphanages, motels, schools (*madrasahs*), Sufi lodges (*zawiyat*), water wells, food distribution, debt relief and other forms of social welfare (Baer 1997; Hasan 2006).

The nationalisation of society: can waqfs be revived?

In time, this independent social welfare sector deteriorated and the waqf system became an official institution, which was centralised under the state and separate from the private waqfs (*waqf ahliy* or family waqf) (Lewis 1990). The waqfs were administrated by society led by the *'ulama'* (religious scholars)[2] since the early years of Islam. Waqfs have performed an important role in Muslim societies throughout history and throughout Muslim nations in establishing and sustaining educational institutions including prominent higher education institutions such as the al-Qurawiyun University in Tunisia, al-Azhar in Cairo and other

2 Ulama or the scholars and experts of the science of Islam have a special place in the heart of Muslims and within the social strata of the community. As people who possess the knowledge of revelation and as the guardians of the religion through the preservation of the Quran and its traditions, the Quran glorifies the status of ulama. Ulama emerged as an institution separate from the state but as an essential part of Muslim civil society to become the guardians of religion on behalf of the society free from interference of the Caliph or the state (Imarah 2005: 84–92).

early universities in Islamic Andalusia – all long before Oxford and Cambridge were established (Baer 1997). They also built hospitals and clinics throughout Muslim lands, which were known as *bimaristan* thus contributing to the enhancement of medical science and discoveries by Muslim scientists (ibid.). One would conclude that due to the vast and wide practice of waqf throughout Muslim history, individuals and society have been empowered, hence minimising the role of state in education, welfare and even healthcare.

Unfortunately, after the colonial period, when waqfs became institutions of the state, they ceased to have a dynamic role in society. The official role of waqfs was relegated to being strongly associated with religious matters (mosques, cemeteries, orphanages, madrasahs, maintenance of religious authorities, etc.) with some emphasis in a few Muslim countries on other charity and welfare issues (Lewis 1990; Baer 1997). Similarly, non-official waqfs, such as family waqfs, were also affected by the involvement of the state. However, the emergence of Islamic movements, organisations and the *da'wah* (Islamic Propagation) and other progressive groups in the forms of non-governmental organisations (NGOs), quasi-NGOs and foundations has established a new revival of the waqf as a citizen-based charity and welfare movement (see, for example, Clark 1995; Lapidus 1996).

Waqfs, as they functioned in the past, should be an important institution within the ideal independent non-state welfare system. With a constructive role in providing revenue for civil society, waqfs could fuel the sense of empowerment of individuals and, accordingly, constantly cultivate an atmosphere of benevolence in society, hence helping once again to detach society from the state.

Cizakca (2004) has proposed a model through which the concept of a 'cash waqf' can be used in contemporary times to serve the objectives of society using his experience of Muslims involved in microfinance in Turkey during the Ottoman period. Under this practice, established entrepreneurs helped new entrepreneurs by providing them with capital taken from a waqf fund contributed by the established entrepreneurs. Without any assistance from the state, this approach was effective in expanding the culture of business and entrepreneurship among the Ottoman Turkish community. It helped to enhance entrepreneurship within society and reduced the role of the state and, at the same time, enhanced the element of benevolence within the community, hence leading to the nourishment of the ihsani culture (Cizakca 2004).

An effective minimal state

In their proposal for an efficient Islamic economic system, El-Ashker and Wilson (2006: 400) maintain that a politically strong Islamic state is among the essentials for the establishment of an Islamic economy soundly grounded in a strong moral order. In the same vein, Chapra (1992: 240) accepts that the political structure is one of the most important factors responsible for the failure of Muslim countries to implement the Islamic strategy for development with justice. It should be noted that Zaman and Asutay (2009: 92–93) warn that what is meant by politics or the political establishment is not always synonymous with the state or government-led establishment. They highlight the role of civil society as another important factor in the political structure. Furthermore, they argue that the state is a modern post-Enlightenment Western concept and hence is not inherently an appropriate Islamic organisation for political society.

The nature of modern states is also highlighted by the Virginia School of Political Economy, which argues that the state should not be seen in a romantic sense to serve society and maximise a romantically constructed social welfare function. In any case, even if such a social welfare function existed, there are no 'benevolent despotic' politicians to maximise such a welfare function (Zaman and Asutay 2009: 93).

The state should be 'minimal' and 'limited' in nature to allow the other representatives of society to have their share in power and decision-making. The state in early Islam was exemplified by the Prophet Muhammad during his reign in Medina and by the Caliphs. It functioned as the protector of people, of their security and of their freedom. It maintained law and order and regulated the market and public goods without interfering in the market process through central planning. The state was the guardian of the conditions in which the individuals could act according to their beliefs. However, under the succeeding dynasties and sultanate regimes, the state became too large and was expected to undertake public works, be guardian of the religion and govern the life of the people. In exchange it demanded the obedience of the people (Lambton 1981: 308–9; Kahf 1991; see also An-Naim 2008).

Islamic governance in an ideal state will not dominate the centre but rather empower the peripheries to enable individuals to function and thus have greater involvement in the public sphere. Apart from its limited nature, the state also plays an important role as regulator and enforcer in creating a just order and harmonious society through the implementation of the rule of law and its mechanisms that demand the separation of powers. In turn, this entails an independent judiciary, institutional checks and balances and effective watchdogs that can all restrain arbitrary state action and corruption.

It is such a state with limited powers that enables individuals, society and social institutions to function and be independently self-governing – including in the field of welfare provision. A benevolent society should operate philanthropically through the waqf mechanism, which is based on the ideals of property rights and individual ownership. The waqf ensures the social and economic independence of individuals and society through the maintenance of a sustainable system, which will contribute towards strengthening civil society and thereby shrinking the burden on the state

(Zarqa 1988). Consequently, civil society will be able to assume responsibility for social and economic development including the provision of education, public health and so on.

Conclusion

There needs to be a new paradigm for government so that the independent welfare institutions from Islamic history can re-emerge in a new form. New non-state welfare institutions akin to earlier models should be developed with appropriate adjustment to the modern situation to make the ideal workable today.

The waqfs should re-emerge as independent endowment foundations as part of the third sector in the context of a government that plays a smaller role in the economy. Their purpose should be to fund welfare and other civil society activity whilst removing individuals' reliance on the state. This proactive role of the waqfs will strengthen the third sector to stimulate the welfare system, hence empowering the development of ihsani social capital so as to create an opportunity for the emergence of both active citizens and a benevolent society. In achieving such an aim, the waqf has to be separated from the state and be expanded into a larger dynamic form.

The state's role is to enable individuals to function and institutions to flourish and be self-reliant within a benevolent society, thus leading the way to citizens exercising their rights and responsibilities.

It should also be noted that this requires a decentralised state with power vested in local communities. Historical experience shows that, when Muslim empires pursued decentralised administration, they provided a very large space for civil society and social institutions to actively function and contribute to the development of non-state welfare institutions. Such a decentralised state will ensure the separation of powers, leading towards an independent and effective societal-based mutual cooperation.

If the state stops dominating every aspect of the individual's life, such a decentralised state will motivate and enable a more efficient and stronger role for civil society to help administer the social, economic and political lives of the people. The civil society institutions of the past, such as waqf, were nourished due to the nature of the decentralised state in some periods of Muslim history. In reflecting on the historical experience, it is obvious that the decentralised nature of administration in every sphere of life brought about a strong society with a flourishing civil society.

Moreover, this reform agenda, and the development of waqfs as a vehicle for the creation of a benevolent society, will lead to a higher level of independence among the people, hence minimising the perceived need for a big state. This is one of the prerequisites for development. The nature of civil society institutions can be described as 'the realm of organised social life that is voluntary, self-generating, (largely) self-supporting, autonomous from the state, and bound by a legal order or a set of shared rules' (Ghaus-Pasha 2005: 1–2). Thus the state's role is to provide the legal order (if that is necessary) but the civil society institutions help provide order and structure in society in a way that is independent of the state.

In explaining the nature of the alternative non-state welfare system based on Islamic ideals of common justice and fairness, it must be made clear that the benevolent society must be based on the promotion of the dignity of the human person, the inviolability of life and freedom used responsibly. This involves embracing Islamic values, spirituality and the horizontal–vertical moral precepts among the members of society in order to promote the moral and material uplifting of individuals, thereby motivating them to achieve the noble goals taught by the religion.

The non-state welfare system would also cultivate the widespread accumulation of social, human, cultural and natural capital that is essential for development. This should involve widespread humanistic elements (education, health, skills, ownership and lifestyle), social aspects (networking, rules of society, solidarity and welfare) and cultural aspects (social relations, customs and structures), which have all been acknowledged as an active contributor to economic development, good governance and stable democracies (Kliksberg 2001).

Meanwhile, at the micro level, the interrelated elements of Tawhidi ontology cultivate the norms of self-determination, including respect for life, self-respect, justice and equity, mutual respect, caring, sharing and integrity.

The whole process of this ideal welfare system, which will remove the obstacles to the nourishment of a truthful human life in which all members of society are able to develop their human capacity in order to obtain personal and social well-being, is but another version of '*jihad fi sabil Allah*' (striving in the way of Allah).

References

An-Na'im, A. A. (2008) *Islam and the Secular State: Negotiating the Future of Shari'a*. Harvard University Press.

Baer, G. (1997) The *waqf* as a prop for the social system (sixteenth-twentieth centuries). *Islamic Law and Society* 4(3): 264–97.

Baskan, B. (2002) Waqf system as a redistribution mechanism in Ottoman Empire. Northwestern University, Department of Political Science.

Chang, H. N. (1997) Democracy, diversity and social capital. *National Civic Review* 86(2): 141–47.

Chapra, M. U. (1992) *Islam and the Economic Challenge*. Leicester: The Islamic Foundation.

Cizakca, M. (2004) *Ottoman Cash Waqf Revisited: The Case of Bursa 1555–1823*. Manchester: Foundation for Science Technology and Civilization.

Clark, J. A. (1995) Islamic social welfare organisations in Cairo: Islamization from below? *Arab Studies Quarterly* 17(4): 11–17.

El-Ashker, A. A. F. and Wilson, R. (2006) *Islamic Economics: A Short History*. Leiden: Brill.

Ghaus-Pasha, A. (2005) Role of civil society in governance. Paper presented at the Sixth Global Forum on Reinventing Government, 24–27 May, Seoul, South Korea.

Gil, M. (1998) The earliest *waqf* foundations. *Journal of Near Eastern Studies* 57(2): 125–40.

Hasan, S. (2006) Muslim philanthropy and social security: prospects, practices, and pitfalls. Paper presented at the 6th International Society for Third-Sector Research (ISTR) Biennial Conference, 9–12 July, Bangkok, Thailand.

Hoexter, M. (1998) *Waqf* studies in the twentieth century: the state of the art. *Journal of the Economic and Social History of the Orient* 41: 476–95.

Ibn Manzur, M. bin M. (1956) *Lisaan al-'Arab*. Beirut: Dar Saadir.

Imarah, M. (2005) *Al-Islaam wa Huquq al-Insaan* [Islam and Human Rights]. Damascus: Dar al-Salaam.

Kahf, M. (1991) The economic role of state in Islam. Lecture Presented at the Seminar on Islamic Economics in Dakka, Bangladesh. http://monzer.kahf.com/papers/english/economic_role_of_state_in_islam.pdf (accessed 1 August 2010).

Keane, J. (2009) *The Life and Death of Democracy*. London: Simon & Schuster.

Kliksberg, B. (2001) *Towards an Intelligent State*. International Institute of Administrative Sciences. Amsterdam, The Netherlands: IOS Press.

Lambton, A. K. S. (1981) *State and Government in Medieval Islam: An Introduction to the Study of Islamic Political Theory: The Jurists, London Oriental Series*, Volume 36. Oxford University Press.

Lapidus, I. M. (1996) State & religion in Islamic societies. *Past & Present* 151(1): 3–27.

Lewis, B. (1990) State and civil society under Islam. *New Perspectives Quarterly* 7(2): 38–41.

Malik, M. (2011) Constructing the architectonics and formulating the articulation of Islamic governance: a discursive attempt in Islamic epistemology. PhD thesis, Durham University, http://etheses.dur.ac.uk/832/ (accessed 31 January 2013).

Malik, M. (2014) Ihsani social capital: a conceptual exploration to faith-inspired social capital. *International Journal of Education and Social Science* 1(2): 62–68.

Newton, K. (1997) Social capital and democracy. *American Behavioral Scientist* (March–April): 575–86.

Taleqani, A. M. (1986) Jihad and Shahadat. In *Jihad and Shahadat: Struggle and Martyrdom in Islam* (ed. M. Abedi and G. Legenhausen). North Haledon and New Jersey: Islamic Publications International.

Wehr, H. (1979) *A Dictionary of Modern Written Arabic* (ed. J. M. Cohen). Wiesbaden: Otto Harrassowitz.

World Bank (1999) What is social capital? Available at http://www.world bank.org/poverty/scapital/whatsc.htm (accessed 10 January 2010).

Zaman, N. and Asutay, M. (2009) Divergence between aspirations and realities of Islamic economies: a political economy approach to bridging the divide. *IIUM Journal of Economics and Management* 17(1): 73–96.

Zarqa, M. A. (1988) Islamic distributive schemes. In *Distributive Justice and Need Fulfillment in an Islamic Economy* (ed. M. Iqbal), pp. 163–216. Leicester: The Islamic Foundation.

5 THE INDIVIDUAL, FREEDOM OF CHOICE AND TOLERANCE IN THE QURAN

Azhar Aslam

Consensus opinion suggests that the philosophies of individualism and liberalism that opened the path to modernity in the West are Western in origin, and that Islamic civilisation opposes and rejects this. Islamic societies are seen as collectivist. This is seen as one of the main reasons why Muslims have failed to assimilate modernity.

This thinking implies that the basis for such a collectivist ideology is in the Quran and this leads to lack of individual initiative in social, economic and political spheres in Islamic societies. Evidence for this is found in those Muslim societies in which there is a lack of freedom in matters of faith and how to live one's life. Orthodox Islamic thought is presented as evidence, with Sharia law (the Muslim legal framework) about apostasy (leaving the Islamic faith) being the prime example.

In this chapter we explore these questions about the individual, freedom of choice (especially in matters of faith) and tolerance within Muslim countries. Our focus here will be on two aspects. Firstly, does the Quran sanction (or even condone) a position where the individual does not have freedom of choice? Secondly, if it is not the scriptural position, why and how have Muslim societies reached the position where there is such lack of tolerance?

The individual in the Quran

The Quran is the primary and the most foundational source of Muslim civilisation. Even a cursory reading of the Quran establishes that God's primary addressee is each individual human person. The Quran places the individual at the very heart of its discourse. The Quran is God's direct conversation with each human person in their individual capacity. In the Quran, God assigns all individuals responsibility of action, and freedom to choose their own actions.

The sentence structure of the Quran may be classified as follows: informative and descriptive statements; declarative statements; imperative statements such as direct commands and exhortations; and questions (addressed to humankind) leading to conclusions. In addition, there are metaphors and similes. Hundreds of examples of morphology and syntax of the Quran leave little doubt that the addressee of God is every human person. The Quran talks to each and every one of us directly; it talks to every woman and every man, every Muslim and every non-Muslim. So if the individual is the addressee of God, how come Islam's dominant outward symbols are unambiguously social, and why is there a perceived imbalance between communal and individual self-interest? There are two obvious reasons for this. Firstly, while addressing individual believers, a good deal of the Quran is devoted to legislation and guidance of the affairs of, as the Quran terms all the believers, 'the middle community', and its collective existence.

The second element that contributed to the gradual erosion of the individual's status in Muslim societies is that the earliest period of Muslim history – the first forty years that are regarded by most Muslims as the ideal they strive for – had social institutions and statecraft as its primary constituents. Subsequently, as Muslim civilisation entered a stage of stagnation and then a stage of decay, the perceived threats to the Umma (the Muslim community) relegated the self-interest of the individual to a secondary position. Human beings are at once individual and social. Each individual lives in the socio-politico-economic framework of his time. Hence, while his actions are his own, they are influenced by and, in turn, influence society. Therefore, although the Quran speaks to each individual human being, the social, political and economic conclusions it draws, and recommendations it makes, are communal in nature.

However, the Quran makes it absolutely clear that actions taken in this world will be judged, and on judgement day the consequences of these actions, reward or punishment, are specific to the individual. No one is responsible for anyone else's actions. The Quran says 'Today [on the day of judgement] you have come to us as individuals [*furada*] just as We created you in the first place' (Surah or Chapter 6, verse 95, denoted as 6:95). Further in 19:80 the Quran states 'He [man] shall come to Us alone [as an individual]'.

Individual responsibility and accountability is unequivocally expressed in the injunction: 'Every soul earns for itself, and no soul shall bear the burden of another, and even thus shall you return to your Lord' (4:165). This is repeated in the Quran 12:15, 25:18, 39:7 and 63:38. In Rehman (1966) the following points are made: 'The ultimate repository of the divine trust is the individual person ... service to God means the sum total of the output of man under the moral law ... The most recurring term in Quran is Taqwa, which attunes man to discharge these responsibilities, is an attribute of the individual and not of society ... while the individual may rely on the collective wisdom of the mankind, he or she is the individual bearer of this responsibility'. The clearest example of this 'individual act leads to communal action' principle is shown in fundamental acts of Muslim worship. A man creates his social being within the collective, but achieves this through his individual actions. A Muslim prays individually but within a collective forum; his individual fast is within the social context; his zakat (alms tax) is his individual effort to help fellow human beings; and finally his individual pilgrimage creates a social movement.

This principle of individual responsibility is the basis on which there is no priesthood between man and his creator, and hence a good individual is the spiritual ideal of Islam.

Iqbal, the greatest Muslim thinker of the twentieth century, states that the main purpose of the Quran is to awaken in man the higher consciousness of his manifold relations with God and the Universe (Iqbal 1934: 6).[1] He further states 'The Quran in its simple, forceful manner emphasizes the individuality and uniqueness of man ... It is in consequence of this view of man as a unique individuality which makes it impossible for one individual to bear the burden of another, and entitles him only to what is due to his own personal effort' (ibid.: 42).

The conclusion is obvious. While the Islamic community has its basis in the Quran, the word of God and the Sunna (the practice) of the Prophet (pbuh), Islamic polity is born through individual Muslims. Similarly, without individual Muslims there is no Islamic economics and there is no Islamic society. As Nehaluddin (2011) observes, no society can survive that does not give first priority to self-interest in individual action; and the whole of the Islamic social, political, religious and spiritual structure is based on a harmony which finds its echo in every Quranic mandate. The socio-economic and political reality of Islamic fabric is built around the individual who discharges the trust that God has placed in him.

Individuals, however, can only discharge this trust if they have complete freedom of choice to make of life what they will, so that they fulfil the trust God has placed in them. Only by allowing freedom of choice and action can an individual Muslim and person be ready to face God on the day of judgement.

---

1   Page numbers to this text are for the web edition (see list of references).

Freedom of individual action and choice in the Quran

The Quran is the primary basis of Islamic law, at least in theory. While the Quran is divine, Sharia is not. And, as we shall see later, political exigencies led scholars to ignore clear Quranic injunctions on some occasions. In the classical period they devised legal edicts based on attributed Hadiths (sayings) of the Prophet, ignoring clear Quranic injunctions. But, for the moment, let us focus on the Quran.

Establishing the Quran's stance in this matter is crucial for two reasons. Firstly, it defines the relations between Muslims and non-Muslims and, secondly, it lays down divine guidance about the legitimacy and tolerance of other faiths.

Study of the Quran shows that there are four themes interwoven within the subject of freedom of choice for an individual. The Quran dealt with this subject on at least 82 occasions. All verses dealing with this subject contain all four themes, explicitly or implicitly, but generally one theme dominates with several subtexts. The Quran, it seems, has not left anything to chance in this matter.

The subtexts include the oneness, and the division of, humankind, and the divine purpose behind this division. They also include the relationship and conduct of believers towards non-believers with particular emphasis on the relationship with 'people of the book'. There are several direct commands to believers regarding their general behaviour in matters of faith.

A detailed study leaves little doubt that God has purposefully treated individual responsibility and freedom of choice as a major issue for the guidance of Muslim believers. The Quran decrees that every individual is free to choose his own course of life in social, economic and political spheres. Further, the Quran stops its followers from challenging another person's freedom of choice.

The first major theme that unambiguously appears repeatedly is that God is the ultimate judge of all human action and everyone will be accountable to God alone. The three other themes are the limitations on the role of the Prophet (pbuh) in enforcing faith, individuals' ownership of their actions, and humans' freedom of choice in respect of their actions and beliefs. This is not the forum to discuss all Quranic verses so we shall limit ourselves to a few examples. Let me start with the final and last-to-be revealed verse of the Quran. This last direct message of God sums up all the main themes and puts a seal on the Quran: 'And be conscious of the Day on which you shall be brought back unto God, whereupon every human being shall be repaid in full for what he has earned, and none shall be wronged' (2:281).

Accountability on judgement day in front of God is the fundamental reason God has sent His word and His prophets. This is the foundational concept of Muslim life and law (Sharia). In fact the *raison d'être* of Sharia is to guide human beings since they are individually accountable to God: 'O you who have attained faith! It is for your own selves that you are responsible: those who go astray can do you no harm if you are on the right path. Unto God you all must return: and then He will make you [truly] understand all that you were doing [in life]' (5:105).

God has kept the right of final judgement to Himself alone. He has given human beings very limited scope to judge each other and only in certain worldly matters, thereby providing freedom to individuals about the course of their lives. The Quran says in 6:61–62: 'And He alone holds sway over His servants ... Oh, verily, His alone is all judgement...'

In the Quran 45:14–15 God says 'Tell all who have attained to faith, that they should forgive those who do not believe in the coming of the Days of God, [since it is] for Him [alone] to requite people for whatever they may have earned. Whoever does what is just and right, does so for his own good; and whoever does evil, does so to his own hurt; and in the end unto your Sustainer you all will be brought back'.

God's command is quite clear. Each person is free to choose and is responsible for his own conduct in life. There will be a judgement day, a responsibility which is God's alone as the ultimate judge. Therefore, coercion is prohibited in this life, and no one has a right to force others to choose how they conduct their life.

Through these direct commandments a direct relationship between God and man is also unequivocally established. This foundational principle has been invoked by Muslims throughout history to stop any one person or establishment accruing too much religious authority, and it has allowed individual Muslims space to challenge authorities that do that. Zubair Khan (2011) says that Islam is an all-embracing idea, and justice is its core value. He elucidates the Quran's message that each individual will stand on their own and the only defence one will have is the good one has done to others.

That God wants everyone to choose freely is made clear in the following injunction, in which God states His will: 'Now had it been our will [that men should not be able to discern between right and wrong], We could surely have deprived them of their sight, so that they would stray forever from the [right] way: for how could they have had insight? And had it been our will [that they should not be free to choose between right and wrong], We could surely have given them a different nature [and created them as beings rooted] in their places, so that they would not be able to move forward, and could not turn back' (36:66–67).

We now turn to the second theme, where God has placed limitations on the Prophet when spreading His message: 'Say [O Prophet]: O mankind! The truth from your Sustainer has now come unto you. Whoever, therefore, chooses to follow the right path, follows it but for his own good; and whoever chooses to go astray, goes but astray to his own hurt. And I am not responsible for your conduct' (10:108).

This verse is specifically addressed to the Prophet (pbuh) and God's command to the Prophet (pbuh) is clear. It is a rule of Sharia that the conduct of the Prophet sets the standard for Muslims to be emulated by each individual believer. The Sunna of the Prophet is the second source of Muslim law and life, after the Quran. All Muslim schools of thought are in agreement that, when God addresses the Prophet, He is making His commandments obligatory to all Muslims.

Muslims are not allowed to exceed the limits set by Prophetic responsibility. In other words our terms and scope of engagement with others cannot be beyond the limits set by God on the Prophet (pbuh). The following verses are unambiguous in the limits set on all Muslims by God Himself when proclaiming the message of the Quran: 'and as for those who turn away We have not sent thee to be their keeper' (4:80); 'hence, We have not made thee their keeper, and neither art thou responsible for their conduct' (6:107).

This command to the Prophet is repeated further in 9:129, 16:82, 26:216, 27:92, 42:48 and 64:12. God is very clear in this matter. The Prophet is told 'thy duty is no more than to deliver the message; and the reckoning is Ours' (13:40).

We now turn to Quranic injunctions regarding individual responsibility. The Quran says 'God does not burden any human being with more than he is well able to bear: in his favour shall be whatever good he does, and against him whatever evil he does' (2:286).

In 6:164 and 39:7 God says 'no bearer of burdens shall be made to bear another's burden. And, in time, unto your Sustainer you all must return: and then He will make you [truly] understand...' This injunction is repeated in 2:134, 2:141 and 41:46.

Finally, we discuss the freedom of choice for an individual. The Quran is most emphatic about each person's freedom to choose their own course of life. In fact this choice has been described as God's will. The following verse shows clearly how God's will acts. It acts through human action and the choices human persons make. According to the Quran it is God's will for humans to hold divergent views (2:253):

> And if God had so willed, they who succeeded those [apostles] would not have contended with one another after all evidence of the truth had come to them; but [as it was,] they did take to divergent views, and some of them attained to faith, while some of them came to deny the truth. Yet if God had so willed, they would not have contended with one another: but God does whatever He wills.

This is repeated in 16:93 'for, had God so willed, He could surely have made you all one single community; ... and you will surely be called to account for all that you ever did!' And again in 32:13: 'Yet had We so willed, We could indeed have imposed Our guidance upon every human being: but [We have not willed it thus – and so]'.

Such freedom of choice is also explicitly given in the following verses: 5:54, 6:104,10:40, 10:41, 17:105–108, 26:4, 28:56 and 39:41. Finally, in 18:29, God says 'And say: The truth [has now come] from your Sustainer: let then him who will, believe in it, and let him who wills, reject it.'

The clear Quranic injunctions regarding apostasy fall within this discussion, but will be discussed below.

No compulsion

We now turn to the most famous, and most often quoted Quranic verse regarding freedom of choice. In 2:256 God says: 'There is no compulsion in *deen* [matters of faith]. Guidance is clear from error'. The verse prohibits the use of compulsion in religion or any other matter of life. The individual has free will and free choice. Islam elevates freedom to such a level that it emphasises free thought as the proper way of recognising God's existence.

Tafsir ibn Kathir,[2] the most famous Sunni exegete of the Quran, explains this verse: 'Do not force anyone to become Muslim, for Islam is plain and clear, and its proofs and evidence are plain and clear. Therefore, there is no need to force anyone to embrace Islam.' Other exegetes agree on this point.

However, there is another aspect of this verse, which is of crucial importance. And that aspect is the positional sequence and placement of the 'no compulsion' verse. This verse, number 2:256, follows verse 2:255, which is the Verse of Throne (*Ayat al-Kursi*). All Muslims know the significance of Ayat al-Kursi, but for the benefit of our non-Muslim readers, this verse is the most often repeated verse after seven verses of Surah Al Fateh, and according to many Hadiths it is the greatest verse of the Quran.

This enhances the importance of the 'no compulsion' verse even more. It is clear that freedom in matters of faith is so crucial to God that He placed the 'no compulsion' command immediately after the declaration of His absolute authority and sway He holds over everything. 'No compulsion' is not a simple 'informational statement' but rather a direct commandment to be absolutely obeyed, with the full force of God's own sovereignty behind it. Therefore, for all Muslims it is absolutely fundamental that they obey God's command of 'no compulsion'.

Subtexts

We now turn to various subtexts that are discussed within all these themes. First and foremost, there is a purpose behind why human beings differ. According to the Quran this divine purpose is to test human persons in the performance of good works: 'for, every community faces a direction of its own, of which He is the focal point. Vie, therefore, with one another in doing good works.

---

2   The English translation is available online with the original Arabic: http://www
    .qtafsir.com/index.php?option=com_content&task=view&id=138.

Wherever you may be, God will gather you all unto Himself: for, verily, God has the power to will anything' (2:147–48).

In 5:48 the Quran tells us: 'Unto every one of you have We appointed a [different] law and way of life. And if God had so willed, He could surely have made you all one single community: but [He willed it otherwise] in order to test you by means of what He has vouchsafed unto, you. Vie, then, with one another in doing good works! Unto God you all must return; and then He will make you truly understand all that on which you were wont to differ.'

This theme is emphasised again in various verses, for example, in 11:117–18, where the Quran says: 'And had thy Sustainer so willed, He could surely have made all mankind one single community: but [He willed it otherwise, and so] they continue to hold divergent views.'

Here we start seeing the glimpses of the legitimacy the Quran provides to non-Muslims and their way of life. But it does not stop there. In one of the earliest revelations to the Prophet (known as a Meccan Surah) God commanded the Prophet to say to the pagans of Mecca: 'Unto you, your moral law, and unto me, mine!' (109:6). The Quran further elaborates on how to respond to non-believers, especially those who mock and make fun. It says: 'And, indeed, He has enjoined upon you in this divine writ that whenever you hear people deny the truth of God's messages and mock at them, you shall avoid their company until they begin to talk of other things' (4:140).

The Quran exhorts believers that God will make the final judgement. These messages are repeated in 10:15, 10:16, 10:17, 10:18 and 15:2.

In 15:3 the Quran says about non-believers: 'Leave them alone ... for in time they will come to know [the truth].' This commandment to leave the non-believers alone is repeated several times in 25:63, 43:83, 43:84, 52:45 and 70:42, where the Quran says: 'Hence, leave them to indulge in idle talk and play [with words] until they face that [Judgement] Day of theirs which they have been promised.'

Quranic instructions regarding the 'people of the book' are even more clear. In 2:62 the Quran tells us: 'Verily, those who have attained to faith [in this divine writ], as well as those who follow the Jewish faith, and the Christians, and the Sabians – all who believe in God and the Last Day and do righteous deeds – shall have their reward with their Sustainer; and no fear need they have, and neither shall they grieve.'

These exhortations are repeated and the Quran is clear how good people of 'the book' will be rewarded. In 3:199 the Quran says: 'And, behold, among the followers of earlier revelation there are indeed such as [truly] believe in God ... Standing in awe of God, they do not barter away God's messages for a trifling gain. They shall have their reward with their Sustainer – for, behold, God is swift in reckoning!'

The Prophet's Sunna

Having seen how the Quran treats the matter of faith and individual freedom, the question arises, if the Quran is so explicit, why the apparent intolerance in Muslim law? The answer to this conundrum lies in Muslim history. But before we explore this question further, it is important to also see the Prophet's Sunna regarding other faiths, because, after the Quran, that is the second source of Islamic civilisation and law.

The first community in Medina was an all-inclusive community. The Prophet (pbuh) explicitly wrote down the first constitution which regulated the affairs of people living in Medina, including Muslims and Jews. Zuabiar Khan refers to the constitution of Medina which stated in article 25: 'The Jews of Banu 'Avf are a community (umma) along with the believers. To the Jews their religion and way of life (deen) and to the Muslims their deen'. Dr Abdullah quotes Watt and says that the treaty not only gave this right but also regarded the Jews as partners with Muslims (Watt 1956: 221–28).

Similarly, the Prophet's Sunna on how he treated Christians is exemplified in his conduct towards the delegation of Christians from Najran (southern Arabia). He received them in his house, entertained them in his mosque and concluded a treaty with them. Similar peace treaties were concluded by his immediate political successors, particularly the second caliph, Umar. He set a great example in the conquest of Jerusalem by refusing to pray in a church, saying, 'I do not want Muslims to start converting churches into mosques after me'. The Christian Patriarch of Mery said: 'The Arabs who have been given by God the Kingdom [of the earth] do not attack the Christian faith; on the contrary they help us in our religion; they respect our God and our Saints and bestow gifts on our churches and monasteries' (Syed Ameer Ali 1997, quoted by Nehal ud Din). Christians enjoyed respect, liberty and a new dignity they had not enjoyed under either Christian Rome or Byzantium. Even later on we see that Christians lived in peace and prospered under Islam for centuries.

According to Thomas Arnold, had it been a part of Islamic sentiment to do away with the Christian presence, it could have been done without a ripple in world history. John Morrow, talking about the conquest of Spain, quotes Ahmad Thomson: 'The oppressed majority of this corrupt and decaying society regarded the Muslims not so much as conquerors but as saviours. The Muslims ended their slavery and gave them freedom to practice their religion' (Morrow 2013: 189).

Islam and the state

Now we turn to our question of why the present Sharia law treats freedom of faith differently from how the Quran commands and the Sunna demonstrates.

Firstly, Sharia is not divine. It is a human construct. It is very important to understand this. The Muslim people tend to treat

Sharia as divine due to a lack of knowledge and understanding. But, when Western intellectuals and the media discuss these matters, particularly in the context of Muslim populations living in the West, they have a responsibility to explain that Sharia law is a law based on divine revelation, but not divine in itself.

It would also not go amiss if the Western media were to at least accept openly, if not emphasise, the Islamic origin of much Western thought. As the respected medieval scholar George Makdisi asserts: 'our religious monotheism is Judeo-Christian, and our intellectual culture is Greco-Roman, what I believe we have yet to realise is that an essential part of our intellectual culture, namely, our university and scholarly culture, is Arabo-Islamic'. Such awareness is crucial to the promotion of tolerance and peace within the West.

Fiqh for Sharia developed within the particular context of an embryonic Muslim empire, and was devised as a simple set of rules to allow Muslims to live according to Islam. Later on, however, it was elevated to the level of the divine, not to be questioned or altered. Those with vested interests, financial and political, continue to perpetuate and support this idea of divine Sharia. The dichotomy that facilitates this is the fact that Islam does not envisage a specific territorial state, and definitely not a nation state, but rather creates a community across borders.

The Quran and the Prophet did not provide any clear instructions or guidelines about statecraft. In fact, the books of Hadith and Fiqh do not have any specific chapters covering these matters. Muhammad Khalid Masud has pointed out that, had the Prophet regarded the state as the ultimate goal, he would have accepted the offer of the Meccan elite to assume chieftainship. In his opinion, 'books and treatises [which] were written later on statecraft ... were either informed by the precedents from Islamic history or derived from the Sassanian model'.

Islamic civil society was based on the rule of law. Although Muslim societies accepted empires and states, the rulers were always seen with suspicion. Royal courts were avoided by scholars and the Prophet's saying, 'speaking truth in front of a tyrant is the greatest jihad', gained currency. The pious declined appointments in governments. Muslims led by scholars, merchants and professionals had decided that their interests were served better with a society independent of the state. The state was viewed as an essential evil, and accepted as the least worst alternative to anarchy and chaos (*fitnaa* and *fassad*).

Slowly and gradually the exigencies of politics, led by dynastic emperorship and expanding Muslim empires, bordered by non-Muslim empires, led scholars to develop the theory of 'Dar al-Islam' (the house of Islam). This major shift resulted in changing Islam from a way of life based on justice, equity, the rule of law and individual freedom into an exclusive territorial and religious empire. The law of apostasy created in this milieu was a political construct, as we will discuss later.

Morrow (2013: 188) observes: 'it is equally evident that the suppression of material that was favourable towards Christians took place at a time when ties between the followers of Christ and followers of Muhammad had degenerated. It appears that a hardening of the positions [occurred] ... with the Muslim scholars becoming increasingly intransigent in their interpretations of Islam rendering the Muslim religion increasingly intolerant, puritanical and exclusivist ... regardless Muslims are duty bound to abide by the example of the Prophet ... The teachings and actions of messenger of Allah speak for themselves'.

Tolerance and the present-day state of Muslim societies

Tolerance in present-day Muslim societies is at its lowest. While outsiders continue to see it as a freedom-of-faith and apostasy issue, the problem of intolerance is more widespread and complex, and goes beyond issues of faith.

Three factors largely explain attitudes in Muslim societies. Firstly, there has been an intellectual vacuum and a failure of Muslim modernists to explain the case for a free society. Iqbal identified three things humanity needs: a spiritual interpretation of the universe; spiritual emancipation of the individual; and basic principles directing the evolution of human society on a spiritual basis. After World War II, it was envisaged that the independence of Muslim countries would bring about the intellectual revival of Islam, which would lead humanity into new vistas and adventures.

This did not happen and there was domination by decadent theocratic forces. The failure of Muslim intellectuals is perhaps the most important explanation for where Muslims stand today. Muslim reformists have never enjoyed political support and, despite a broad social acceptance of their views, have been mostly marginalised. However, reformists themselves have to share the blame for not being bold enough in standing up for their ideas.

Sardar (2011: 1) notes:

> Far from being a liberating force, a kinetic social, cultural and intellectual dynamics for equality, justice and humane values, Islam seems to have acquired a pathological strain. Indeed, it seems to me that we have internalised all those historic and contemporary western representations of Islam and Muslims that have been demonising us for centuries.

He continues that the problem exists because of the elevation of the Sharia to the level of the divine, with the consequent removal of agency from the believers, and the equation of Islam with the state.

A further reason why tolerant voices have not had great influence is because of politics. Factors ranging from the after-effects of colonialism, post-colonial despotism, present-day Western hegemony, attacks on Muslim lands during the past quarter of a century, and Muslims living in an interconnected global society, with burgeoning populations have all resulted in the resurgence of reactionary theories of Islamic statehood, based on a false premise. But, because they promise a land of milk and honey to the have-nots, they attract followers. Morrow (2013: 63) points out that 'the periods of greatest intolerance (in Muslim societies) have coincided with Western imperialist occupation, both past and present.'

This state of affairs is further encouraged by rulers of Muslim countries who suffer from a lack of vision. With rampant corruption and crony capitalism, democracy is mere electioneering with elites exploiting resources for personal gain. Such rulers, often supported by short-sighted Western governments, show no interest in improving the social, political and intellectual lot of Muslim people. There is an unholy alliance of orthodox Mullah and the monopolistic elite. This alliance continues to perpetuate the inbreeding of poverty, lack of education and extremist interpretations of Islam.

Ayoub (1994) states: 'the post-colonial state in Muslim societies has done little to encourage debate in the area of Islamic law. The increased interest in adopting legal codes based in Islamic values leaves the majority of Muslims with outdated legal codes'. He expands further that 'with the marginalization of Islamic juristic learning and the restriction of public debate on Islamic law by the state ... the most rigid and literalist interpretation of Islamic sources prevails, while enlightened and reformist views are suppressed and marginalized.'

Finally, and encouraging the above trends, are socio-economic factors including abject poverty, lack of education, opportunity and justice, and human misery, aggravated by natural and man-made disasters. Hungry stomachs are easily fed with extremist ideas which present Sharia as a panacea for all ills. The elevation of the Sharia to the divine level ensures that people themselves have no opinion or contribution to make, except to follow.

Apostasy

This discussion of liberal thought in Islamic societies is not complete without a discussion of apostasy. It is significant that the Quran refers to apostasy several times (2:217, 3:86–90, 4:137, 9:66, 9:74, 16:106–9, 4:88–91 and 47:25–27) and yet does not prescribe any punishment for it. The former Chief Justice of Pakistan, S. A. Rahman, has written that there is no reference to the death penalty in any of the 20 instances where apostasy is mentioned in the Quran.

The Quran says in 4:115: 'But as for him who, after guidance has been vouchsafed to him, cuts himself off from the Apostle and follows a path other than that of the believers – him shall We leave unto that which he himself has chosen, and shall cause him to endure hell: and how evil a journey's end!' This is clearly a reference to those who left the fold of Islam in the Prophet's lifetime; and it is clearly a reference to God being the judge in the life hereafter. The following verse goes even further and talks about those who apostatised more than once. It also clearly implies that such people lived among Muslims and re-entered the fold of Islam before apostatising once again: 'Behold, as for those who come to believe, and then deny the truth, and again come to believe, and again deny the truth, and thereafter grow stubborn in their denial of the truth – God will not forgive them, nor will He guide them in any way' (4:137–38).

God's punishment for such people is very clear, that, as a result of their repeated apostasy, He will not forgive them. God has not allowed anyone to take matters into their own hands. In 16:106–7 the Quran again talks about those who apostatise and makes it clear that such people will face punishment in the afterlife.

Shafaat (2006) argues that, had the Quran not mentioned apostasy at all, we could have perhaps argued that there was no occasion for the Quranic revelation to deal with this subject and it was therefore left for the Holy Prophet to deal with. He observes that almost all the verses that refer to apostasy are found in the Madinan period, when the Islamic state had been established and penalties for crimes could be prescribed and applied. He concludes that the absence of any legal penalty for apostasy in the Quran means that God never intended any such penalty to become part of Islamic Sharia.

When we look at the Prophet's life we see no concrete evidence of the Prophet prescribing the death penalty for those who left Islam. The Prophet, for example, drew up the Treaty of Hudaybiyya with his Meccan opponents. One of the terms of that treaty was that if a Muslim repudiated Islam and wanted to be with the Meccans, he was permitted to do so.

Ayoub (1994) discusses, in some detail, the traditions from the life of the Prophet that are used by the proponents of the death penalty to justify the death penalty for apostasy. He concludes: 'we have in reality not six, but four traditions, only two of which contain Prophetic injunctions. But even these cannot, as we have seen, serve as material sources for the harsh law.'

So what happened? Apostasy is a political construct. In present-day Muslim societies it is seen as divine only because Sharia is (wrongly) seen as divine. Sharia is now a system of closed corpus which only a few individuals have the right to interpret, and to create rules and regulations. Apostasy and blasphemy have become political weapons in the hands of political groups to be used as a means to eliminate rivals and opponents.

According to Roald (2011): 'The Muslims were in majority and had to keep up this majority in relation to Christians and Jews.' Several arguments can be advanced in support of this thesis. Firstly there is a wide range of opinions about the issue of apostasy, with even the earliest jurists differing widely. Ibrahim Syed argues that this lack of unanimity is the reason 'why some scholars distinguished between individual apostasy and apostasy which is accompanied by high treason.'

Syed further argues[3] that 'a number of Islamic scholars from past centuries including Ibrahim al-Naka'I, Sufyan al-Thawri … have all held that apostasy is a serious sin, but not one that requires the death penalty. In modern times, Mahmud Shaltut, Sheikh of al-Azhar, and Dr Tantawi have concurred'. Ayoub (1994) concludes his analysis by pointing out: 'a careful study of the early sources of Islamic tradition reveals an increasingly hardening attitude towards apostasy … because contradictory views have been attributed to early traditionists, including the founders of the legal schools, later jurists have been free to interpret the classical tradition to fit their own temperament and the time and political climate in which they lived'.

Saeed (2004: 98), in an important book on apostasy, quotes Rached Ghannouchi as saying that apostasy is a political crime and that Quranic evidence asserts principles of freedom of belief and forbids compulsion.

The relief provided to women and minors is also evidence that those designing apostasy laws had political expediency in mind. Sulayman (2011), in his book *Tolerance and Coercion in Islam*, concludes that it was the fighting men who were held accountable for their acceptance or non-acceptance of Islam. Friedman (2003) sums up the views and arguments of Abu Hanifa, the first and the greatest of the four Sunni imams. He states: 'Thus, in Abu Hanifa's analysis, apostasy has two aspects. It is a religious transgression to be punished by God in the hereafter; it is also a political crime, likely to be followed by rebellion' (Friedman 2003: 137). In Friedman's analysis, Abu Hanifa's perception is that apostasy of male Muslims is primarily a political crime, entailing a danger of rebellion. The severe punishment it carries is a matter of public policy, designed to protect the well-being of the Muslim state.

---

3   http://www.irfi.org/articles/articles_251_300/is_killing_an_apostate_in_the_is.htm

According to Ayoub (1994), apostasy remained a theoretical issue for Muslims until very recently and came to the fore as a political question with the rise of Western colonialism. He suggests that the issue is rooted in, and influenced by, the forced secularisation of Muslim society, and the absence of a free debate under the authoritarian regimes that dominate much of the Muslim world.

Conclusion

Islam has established a direct relationship between human persons and God. The Quran and Sunna are absolutely clear about freedom in matters of faith. If we accept the modern view of democracy as not so much participation of the individual in political power, but as a system of protection of the individual from the violence and coercion of the state, Islam's view point is closest to modernity. Islam not only wants freedom of the individual from theocracy, but also from control by the state. Islam emphasises the role and responsibility of the individual and freedom of faith is a fundamental principle.

While, without doubt, Islam makes a distinction between believers and non-believers, the Quran addresses all human persons and envisages a better world and a better humanity by placing the responsibility for action squarely on each individual human being.

Subsequent developments in Sharia law were driven by political interests, as was its promotion to divine status. Muslim lands lie under the stranglehold of corrupt political and theocratic elites and suffer from complex and multifarious troubles. However, none of these problems is insurmountable and the key to revival and reform lies in education of the Muslim peoples along with concerted efforts by intellectuals.

One question, which can only be touched on very briefly, is whether the secularisation of Muslim societies is a solution.

Secularisation, tried both forcefully and by stealth, has failed to a large degree. Firstly, secularism has as its basis the division between the Lord and Caesar held as absolute by some Christians. This division is anathema to Islam. Secondly, Christian societies did not have a glorious past to which they could look back as Muslims do. Thirdly, and perhaps most importantly, Islam provides a great anchoring point of identity to the self, when faced with the dislocating trauma of modernity and globalisation.

A revival must start at the intellectual level with a fresh examination of Sharia in the light of Quranic evidence. To change Muslim societies, and to align them with the original ethos of the Quran and the Sunna, one has to adopt a multi-pronged strategy with intellectual efforts going hand-in-hand with social, political and, most importantly, economic improvements. Change, though, has to be internalised and to come from within. Any outside interference has proved to, and will continue to, aggravate the situation.

Education is the key to this social, political and economic change. Literacy and education will allow Muslims to learn for themselves what the Quran and the Sunna say, rather than depending upon interpretations of others. Intellectuals have to lead this movement and accept the risks such leadership will involve. The easiest task is providing the theoretical basis: that is readily available in the Quran and Sunna, which speak loudly and clearly.

References

Ahmad, N. (2011) The concept of collectivism in relation to Islamic and contemporary jurisprudence. *Open Law Journal* 4: 15–20.

Arnold, T. (1906) *The Preaching of Islam*. London: Constable and Company. (1961, Lahore: Muhammad Ashraf Publications.)

Ayoub, M. (1994) Religious freedom and the law of apostasy. *Islam Islamiyat Masihiyat* 20: 75–91.

Friedman, Y. (2003) *Tolerance and Coercian in Islam. Interfaith Relations in Muslim Tradition.* Cambridge University Press.

Goitein, S. D. (1977) Individualism and conformity in classical Islam. In *Individualism and Conformity in Classical Islam* (ed. A. Banani and S. Vryonis Jr), p. 3. Fifth Giorgio Levi Delia Vida Biennial Conference. Wiesbaden.

Iqbal, A. M. (1934) *The Reconstruction of Religion Thought in Islam.* Oxford University Press. (Web PDF available at www.ziarat.com.)

Khan, Z. Z. (2011) Pluralism in Islam. *Islam and Muslim Societies* 4(2). (Available at http://www.muslimsocieties.org.)

Makdisi, G. (1989) Scholasticism and humanism in classical Islam and the Christian West. *Journal of the American Oriental Society* 109: 175–82.

Masud, M. K. (1993) Civil society in Islam. Presented at a seminar on Islam and Modernity, Karachi, 4–6 November 1993. (Available at www.dkxhtdd7qzxyg.cloudfront.net/27t9bh_civil-islam.pdf.)

Morrow, J. A. (2013) *The Covenants of the Prophet Muhammad with the Christians of the World.* Sophia Perennis.

Musah, M. B. (2011) *The Culture of Individualism and Collectivism in Balancing Accountability and Innovation in Education: An Islamic Perspective.* Ontario International Development Agency.

Rahman, S. A. (1986) *Punishment of Apostasy in Islam.* Kazi Publishing.

Rehman, F. ur (1966) The status of the individual in Islam. *Islamic Studies* 5(4).

Rehman, F. ur (1970) Islamic modernism: its scope, method and alternatives. *International Journal of Middle East Studies* 1: 317–30.

Roald, A. S. (2011) Multiculturalism and pluralism in secular society: individual or collective rights? Bergen: Chr. Michelsen Institute.

Saeed, A. and Saeed, H. (2004) *Freedom of Religion, Apostasy and Islam.* London: Ashgate Publishing.

Sardar, Z. ud D. (2011) Rethinking Islam. *Islam and Muslim Societies* 4(2).

Seyit, K. (2006) The paradox of Islam and the challenges of modernity. In *Negotiating the Sacred Blasphemy and Sacrilege in a Multicultural Society* (ed. E. Burns Coleman and K. White). Acton, Australia: ANU E Press.

Shafaat, A. (2006) *The Punishment of Apostasy in Islam*, Part I: *The Qur`anic Perspective*. (Available at www.islamicperspectives.com/ap ostasy1.htm.)

Sulayman, A. (2011) Apostates, Islam & freedom of faith: change of conviction vs change of allegiance (translated by N. Roberts). Herndon, VA: The International Institute of Islamic Thought.

6 ECONOMIC FREEDOM: THE PATH TO WOMEN'S EMANCIPATION IN THE MIDDLE EAST AND NORTH AFRICA (MENA) REGION

Souad Adnane

Countries of the Arab world have signed and ratified UN treaties relating to gender and women's issues. However, there are well-known and long-standing difficulties with regard to women's lack of participation in economic and political life and in civil society. In the Arab world, gender power and gender relations are affected by socio-cultural and religious norms and women are very much excluded from the public sphere and arenas of development.

An aspect of the cultural problems faced by women is the rising violence and conflict in the Arab world which weaken the position of women in many ways. Women and girls are more vulnerable to violence and it is therefore implied that they are in need of the protection of men. Men are portrayed as the natural protectors and women the ones in need of protection; this often implies that home is the safest place for women (Enloe 2014: 30). Unfortunately, the current context in the Arab world entrenches the historical division of the 'public' and 'private' and this results in a reinforcement of the perceived roles and responsibilities of each gender. How can the position of women be advanced in such a context? What kind of policies would help emancipate women in the Arab world?

Using a mixture of women in development and gender and development reasoning, I shall make the case for the importance of promoting economic freedom of women in the Arab world in advancing their status, as well as advancing the general economic growth of their countries. This chapter argues in favour of market-friendly policies which can spur investment in the health and education of girls and hence contribute in changing power structures. Secondly, it makes the case for a 'gender-sensitive' approach that should accompany the market-friendly policies, as much as possible, to reduce the entry barriers that limit women's autonomy and prevent them from benefiting from such opportunities.

Women in development versus gender and development: implications for policy making in the Arab world

The way in which women's issues have been understood has influenced development policy, both internationally and locally, and given rise to a myriad of practices. The first major trend, women in development, 'is associated with the wide range of activities concerning women in the development domain, in which donor agencies, governments and NGOs have become involved since the 1970s' (Ravazi and Miller 1995: 2). The advocates of this approach adopted an economic efficiency argument, making the case for the potential contribution of women to the development process. The approach has had a lasting impact on development policies and practices.

The women in development approach was born in a context where women were identified by policy makers in their roles as mothers and wives. Policies related to women's issues were restricted to social welfare: the 'welfare approach' (ibid.: 3). As a reaction to this general policy environment, women in development was shaped around the liberal feminist idea that 'women's disadvantages stem from stereotyped customary expectations held by men and internalized by women, and promoted through various agencies of socialization' (ibid.: 3). Women in development aimed at breaking down the stereotypes by promoting 'new' roles for women essentially through training and economic empowerment.

The challenges were greater in patriarchal settings such as the Arab world, where a lot of projects and policies aiming at the economic empowerment of women turned into welfare projects. The prevailing socio-cultural norms in the region, societal structures and power relations constrain the economic freedom of women and the opportunities to which they can have access. While projects for women in sub-Saharan Africa to promote their economic role in farming resulted in a positive impact of real empowerment, because in this region, women are the ones responsible for providing food to their families, similar projects did not work in the MENA as men were identified as the main breadwinners in this part of the world (ibid.: 10).

By the late 1970s, women in development advocates and practitioners started to question the then current model (ibid.: 12). Addressing women's issues regardless of the cultural context had not been an efficient strategy. Although women in development research did a lot of important work in terms of analysing women's subordination and its causes and also in giving relevant recommendations to break down the subordination cycle by providing women with more access to resources, its practice has yielded the major shortcoming of dealing with women's subordination in isolation from the very context and the social systems that produced it. This awareness was also promoted by a rising critique within feminist scholarship of the idea of treating women as one homogeneous group regardless of the different contexts in which they lived (ibid.: 12).

By focusing on socio-cultural norms and how the positions of both men and women are forged and sustained, a new paradigm emerged that also served as a general policy framework. The gender and development approach calls for gender-sensitive policies in all fields instead of specific policies or projects directed only to women. The gender language is currently the one used in the policy field and development practices. However, the outputs are not very different from the outputs of the women in development approach, especially in developing countries. The MENA region probably represents the most challenging case in terms of raising the place of women in the process of development, given its complex patriarchal nature in which social, cultural and religious factors simultaneously come into play.

The Beijing declaration and platform for action, adopted during the Fourth World Conference on Women in 1995, and reaffirmed by the UN in 2000, is the most comprehensive global policy framework that has impacted policy-making as it relates to women around the world including in the MENA region. Looking at the extent of the implementation and compliance with its provisions (by both governments and civil societies) shows the great challenge that MENA countries face. Almost all national reports of Arab countries on the implementation of the Beijing declaration and platform for action twenty years on highlight the challenges related to the cultural environment in those countries. Even where there is legislation and policies that promote gender equality, local contexts in Arab countries respond poorly to them so that a huge gap is created between planning and implementation (UN Women 2015). The conventional role attributed to women – being in the home – restricts their presence in the public sphere.

The rise of armed conflicts and violence in the region has worsened the situation and strengthened the perception of the home as being a safer place for women. Political instability and turmoil in many countries of the region have affected men and women differently. While men are more likely to die in conflicts, women are more likely to experience many forms of sexual violence. Indeed, reports denounce the use of sexual violence to target opponents in Tunisia, Egypt and Syria during the period of unrest that is still ongoing in some areas. Syrian refugees in Jordan, Lebanon, Turkey and Libya tend to marry off their daughters at a young age, believing that marriage will provide them with some form of protection. In Egypt, civil society organisations have reported intense forms of harassment of women in the streets, especially during demonstrations (UN Women 2013: 10). In such contexts, women's freedom of movement is further limited and women are even more confined to the private sphere for protection.

In spite of the gender and development approach, which urged 'gender mainstreaming', projects related to the economic empowerment of women in the MENA region have mainly taken a women-only form. The most recurrent example of women's economic empowerment, and one important pillar in the Beijing Declaration, is income-generating activities. While encouraging women's entrepreneurship is really important, promoting such income-generating activities without the necessary prerequisites would not and does not have the desired impact, in terms of participation and outcomes. As the UN states, there are also 'barriers to service access for rural and poor women, administrative complications; delays in amendments to laws on women's economic independence; the limited access of women to production tools, property ownership and resources' (ibid.). All these problems necessitate policies that are both market friendly and gender sensitive if they are to be overcome.

The economic participation of women in the MENA region

Most Arab countries show a pattern approximating to gender equality in health and education (with women outnumbering men in higher education). This has improved their Human Development Index scores, allowing them to record the world's fastest progress since the 1970s (World Economic Forum 2014). Higher per capita incomes have accompanied this progress in human development. However, these positive developments did not lead to an improvement in women's economic participation as it did in other parts of the world.

This combination of trends is specific to the MENA region and is referred to in World Bank reports as the 'MENA puzzle' (World Bank 2013a). But the puzzle can be solved when we take into account two points. Firstly, there is the problem of the specific patriarchal nature of MENA societies characterised by the segregation between the 'private' and the 'public' that frames and forges gender roles; and, secondly, the specific nature of economic growth in the MENA region stemming basically from rent-seeking economies that do not necessarily promote economic freedom for everyone.

The MENA region records the world's lowest rate of female labour market participation (25 per cent) compared with a global average of 50 per cent. The rate of increase has been very slow. Participation varies from one country to another, from 5 per cent in Yemen to 48 per cent in the United Arab Emirates (see Figure 2, taken from the World Bank Report; ibid.: 39).

Young MENA women also face the highest unemployment rate in the world (nearly 40 per cent compared with 22 per cent among young men) (ibid.). The MENA region also records the lowest regional average score on the Global Gender Gap Index (GGI), with the MENA region's highest-scoring country, Kuwait, being below the regional averages of all the other five regions (Global Gender Gap Report 2014). In spite of the noticeable improvement in health and education (which constitute two of the four subindices of the GGI, economic participation and political empowerment being the other two), the region is still lagging behind with only 60 per cent of its gender gap closed by 2013. Economic participation is the component that most widens the gender gap in MENA countries. Indeed, 'the [MENA] region continues to rank last on the the Economic Participation and Opportunity subindex, with only 42 per cent of the economic gender gap closed' (ibid.).

Figure 2   Female and male labour force participation across MENA

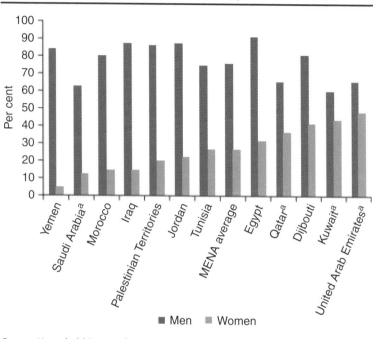

Source: Household Surveys (Appendixes A and C).
[a]Official estimates of nation's non-immigrant population.

The limited level of female labour participation in the MENA region can be explained by a set of interacting factors. Those factors can be summarised as follows:

- Legal restrictions partly reflecting social norms and the limiting of women's autonomy (such as movement).
- Restricted access to assets and finance (bank accounts, loans, land, and so on).
- An unfriendly environment for women wishing to set up a business (such as administrative complications and legal requirements among other things).

Table 2   Global Gender Gap Index (GGI) data for selected MENA countries

Country	GGI score	GGI overall rank (out of a total of 142 countries)	Economic participation subindex (scores and ranks)	Ease of Doing Business Index (World Bank rank out of 189 countries)
Yemen	0.5145	142	0.3596 (138)	137
Saudi Arabia	0.6059	130	0.3893 (137)	49
Morocco	0.5988	133	0.4000 (135)	71
Jordan	0.5968	134	0.3580 (140)	117
Tunisia	0.6272	123	0.4634 (130)	60
Egypt	0.6064	129	0.4609 (131)	112
Qatar	0.6403	116	0.6197 (101)	50
Kuwait	0.6457	113	0.6083 (106)	86
United Arab Emirates	0.6436	115	0.5152 (123)	22

Source: Data collected from the Global Gender Gap Report (2014) and the WB Ease of Doing Business Index (2014).

- An unfriendly environment for businesses that could employ women (tax rates, complicated administrative requirements, fraud, corruption, political instability).
- Onerous labour regulations that lead employers to discriminate against women.
- A mismatch between the skills required by employers and women's educational achievements.
- Socio-cultural norms.

Table 2 shows the the GGI scores of the countries depicted in Figure 2. The table also supports the relevance of some of the above-mentioned factors (data were not available for some countries).

Market-friendly policies and their potential for advancing the position of women in the Arab world

The lack of economic participation by women in the MENA region has important implications for their position within this part of the world. Women's limited access to economic opportunities reduces their resilience and makes them financially dependent on men, which engenders other types of dependence. It also reduces their access to basic needs such as health and education as well as reducing their autonomy.

The fact that the lives of women tend to be lived in the private[1] sphere – a de facto effect of their alienation from the public sphere – increases the likelihood of domestic violence, with more power being in the hands of men and domestic violence being considered as a private matter. Associating the status of women with the private sphere weakens their position within society in general, limiting their individual liberties such as freedom of movement, freedom of expression and decision-making. As mentioned earlier, the private versus public space dichotomy underpins the Arab patriarchy and is very important in understanding the power imbalances and gender inequalities that have shaped, throughout centuries, women's position in the Arab world (Adnane 2013).

The World Bank (2011) highlights how greater access to economic resources improves women's autonomy through increasing their bargaining power and allowing them to accumulate personal assets (physical, personal and financial). Women's control is indeed greater in wealthier households worldwide. The MENA region is not only no exception to this general rule but actually shows a steeper increase in the share of women with some control over decision-making as households become richer (World Bank 2011: 154).

---

1   The word 'private' is used here in the sense of 'not-public' where public means anything that involves public interaction and exposure. Private and public are not used here to mean non-state and state.

The obstacles to economic freedom for women in the MENA region seem to be greater than in any other part of the world. Informal obstacles (socio-cultural) intervene directly in limiting the presence of women in the public sphere, but also make it more difficult for women to overcome formal obstacles to economic participation.

In very many poor and middle-income countries, women are more likely to be intimidated by the huge number of requirements, administrative procedures and the time needed to start a business, and many of them are deterred from doing so. For example, '75% of the world's women cannot get bank loans because they have unpaid or insecure jobs and are not entitled to property ownership' (World Economic Forum 2014). Entrepreneurship among women is particularly low in the Arab world and this is not surprising given the Ease of Doing Business Index scores in Table 2. Arab countries, except for the United Arab Emirates, Qatar and Kuwait, score very low on the index. Not surprisingly, Arab countries also score very low on the 2014 Gender Gap Report.

Kuwait, the United Arab Emirates and Qatar all have among the most market-friendly regulatory regimes in the MENA region and among the highest levels of economic participation by women. In other countries though, where the general policy environment is not market friendly, many people – especially women – find employment in the informal sector.

The existence of a large informal sector is more likely to affect women than men. Indeed, this is a particular problem in the Arab world (World Bank 2011). 'While high-income countries have on average four new firms per 1000 working-age people, MENA countries register only 0.63 new firms, ahead of only sub-Saharan Africa' (UN Women 2012). Although this affects both men and women, the MENA business climate remains particularly hostile to women. A World Bank finding shows, for instance, that 'female-owned firms in Egypt report needing 86 weeks on average to resolve a conflict through the legal system, compared to 54 weeks for male-owned firms' (World Bank 2010). Access to finance, in particular loans, requires collateral in the form of tangible assets and a credit history that women are less likely to possess due to the interplay with other factors (World Bank 2013a).

Jordan is a particular example that shows how the interplay between different policies limits women's economic participation. It is the lowest in the region, despite the 99 per cent female literacy rate. In Jordan, men have social control over economic assets, land, bank accounts, access to loans, and family-related benefits including salaries and pensions. If a woman wants to receive family-based payments directly she has to go through complicated administrative procedures. In addition, women under thirty and previously married women are required to have male guardians to undertake basic procedures such as obtaining a passport. Women's work is restricted in some sectors and during night-time hours both in the public and private sectors (that is, work by women is restricted from 7 p.m. to 6 a.m. except in work places specified by the Ministry of Labour) (World Bank 2013b).

General labour regulations in the MENA region, and also those relevant to women such as maternity benefits, make the region less attractive for investment and women less attractive for employment.

A focus on women's issues, projects, policies or on positive measures to help women does not always have the intended effect or promote economic freedom. They are a double-edged sword that could act against women by making them less attractive to employers. They could be also a blunt sword that has no effect in the prevailing presence of social and cultural norms. More economic freedom, a better climate for business more generally and less regulation would help women both directly (because such measures help the whole population) and indirectly (because such measures are likely to lead to greater prosperity, which, as we have seen, makes it more likely that women can exercise greater autonomy).

Gender-sensitive and market-friendly policies: the way forward

As argued in the previous section, market-friendly policies promote the economic participation of women. However, their impact is limited if they are not gender sensitive and if nothing is done to address socio-cultural norms and structural inequalities. The limitation of market-friendly policies alone is most apparent in the case of Saudi Arabia. Although it is ahead of Qatar in the Ease of Doing Business Index, Saudi Arabia ranks very low in terms of women's economic participation (three points below Qatar). Much of the difference can be be explained by socio-cultural norms and non-economic policies of the government that limit the autonomy of women.

Addressing such problems, as advocated by the gender and development approach, is crucial to improving the economic participation of women in the MENA region. Changes in government policy could certainly help. For example, the elimination of male guardianship, a guarantee of equal treatment before the law, a removal of restrictions on women's freedom of movement, and so on, would change the environment in which women made economic choices. It is important to examine the barriers to the participation of women in the economy throughout the whole policy-making process.

An appreciation of the way in which different sectors of the economy are most likely to have an impact on the the provision of opportunities for women can help provide useful guidance on the sequencing of policy reform. For example, the development of female-friendly sectors may have spillover effects on women's employment as well as on economic growth more generally.

Changing socio-cultural norms that cut across all sectors of MENA societies, including businesses, employers and financial services, is also crucial. Such change should come from within, but should also be promoted by the elimination of state regulations and policies that discriminate against women. Civil society organisations should engage in advocacy to remove such discrimination, to call for equal treatment before the law and to make the case for greater economic freedom. Women's organisations in the MENA region (like the majority of women's organisations around the world) spend too much time and energy advocating for larger welfare programmes that can reinforce a state paternalistic model and the power structures that are part of the problem. If women are dependent upon the state for their income through welfare programmes, the state is, through its paternalistic structures, effectively acting as the breadwinner. If, for some reason, there are cuts to benefits, a woman's situation can become much like that of a widow. Civil society organisations should also push for changes in socio-cultural norms through raising awareness, not in one or two campaigns or a few projects designed only for women, but through bringing into the mainstream the question of the rights of women and their economic freedom. Men and women should be included in this process of raising awareness and the existing social structures should be reconsidered wisely.

Liberalising state regulations to be more market-friendly and more woman-friendly would certainly provide more opportunities for women to work and compete with men, either through employment or self-employment. It would provide a more favourable climate for businesses to invest and employ women and for women to invest and employ themselves. It would also create more opportunities for the financial sector to provide services adapted and tailored to the needs of women with limited resources. Promoting fundamental economic freedoms is certainly one key to the emancipation of women in the MENA region. Increased economic participation of women would lead gradually to a change in relationships between men and women within society more generally, as is illustrated by the increase in the share of women with control over decision-making as income increases.

Women's economic participation in Islam

A final important element to consider is the role of religion. Despite the presence of significant religious minorities, Islam is a major common denominator of the societies in the MENA region. In one way or another, Islam and Islamic culture have shaped socio-cultural norms in the region, especially regarding issues related to women. Religious interpretations are often used to justify cultural practices and shape people's perceptions. Although this topic is not the main focus of this chapter, a brief general overview of the problem is indispensable for a better understanding of the issue of women's economic participation.

In Islamic history, the Prophet's wife, Khadija, is considered to be a great example of a Muslim female entrepreneur. Khadija was a rich businesswoman, well-respected among the members of her tribe. She hired Muhammed, who was not then a prophet, to take care of her business, the caravan trade. She noticed his integrity and trustworthiness and decided to make a proposal of marriage, which he accepted after 'having proved himself when put in charge of a shipment of Khadija's merchandise' (Netton 2008: 344). Khadija was twice widowed when she met Muhammed. She was 40 years old and he was 25 when they got married, and she remained his only wife until she died. She was the source of great financial and moral support to Muhammed when he began his mission as a messenger of God.

Islam does not impose any restriction on women taking part in commercial transactions, and no male authorisation is required. Husbands, fathers, brothers or any other male relatives are not allowed to make use of the property or wealth of women without their prior free consent. Khadija's story is a great example that tells against any restriction on women's economic freedom in the name of Islam. It is also an example that challenges the current gender role division in MENA societies and the implications of that division.

On the other hand, some religious interpretations of the Quran may be taken to oppose or impair women's economic freedom. In the Quran, we read, 'And abide in your houses' (33:33). The verse was originally intended for the Prophet's wives and aimed at protecting them and distinguishing them from other Muslim women (Abu Shokka 1995: 20). The verse was, however, interpreted by mainstream scholars to refer to all Muslim women. In one exegesis of the Quran, among many others, the author claims that Muslim women should abide in their houses and not leave them unless to deal with some emergency. He supports his interpretation by referring to a couple of Hadiths that mean that women should be confined to the private sphere of their homes, and continues to argue that only women of a certain age (i.e. too old to attract men) are allowed to go out to pray at the mosque (Zuhayli 1986: 10). Sheikh Sharawi, who was an Azhar University scholar and a popular and respected religious figure, supported the generalist interpretation of the verse and opposed women working, especially in top government positions or as judges (Darwish 1998). Such interpretations to a great extent inform socio-cultural norms and popular beliefs and attitudes. The issue is complex and cannot be dealt with in a single section, but it should at least be flagged for further research and analysis. Women's economic participation in the MENA region cannot be enhanced without confronting socio-cultural norms fuelled by (and fuelling) religious interpretations.

Conclusion

The large scope of the MENA, which is a very diverse region with each country having its own context, demographic characteristics and cultural specifications, makes it difficult to draw generalisations. However, there are many characteristics of the region that are shared by all the countries. The two major ones are the patriarchal nature of the societies and similar barriers that limit women's economic participation.

Although examples of discrimination differ from one country to another, they would still fall within at least one of the categories summarised above (see pp. 104–5). A set of recommendations for the region could only serve as a general framework given its diverse nature. However, an increase in economic freedom and a reduction in the regulatory burdens surrounding business would clearly provide more opportunities for women to prosper. Furthermore, it is well established that greater autonomy for women tends to rise hand-in-hand with increases in general prosperity. It is not that gender-specific policies are required, more a general environment of economic freedom. However, the sequencing of policies and their implementation should be sensitive to the needs of women.

The gap between education outputs and market labour demands in the MENA must also be addressed. Furthermore, the role of women in Muslim societies will not be transformed until religious interpretations that lead to the development of socio-cultural norms related to women's autonomy and economic participation are addressed.

References

Abu Shokka, A. (1995) *Tahrir Al Mara' fi 'Assr Al Rissala* [Women's Liberation during the Era of the Prophet], Volume 4. Kuwait: Dar Al Qalam.

Adnane, S. (2013) Improving the position of women within mainly Muslim countries. Paper presented at the Second Annual Conference of Istanbul Network for Liberty, 18 May. Available at http://istanbul network.org/improving-the-position-of-women-within-mainly-mu slim-countries-souad-adnane/ (accessed 25 August 2015).

Darwish, A. (1998) Obituary: Sheikh Mohamed Mutwali Sharawi. *The Independent* (London), 19 June.

Enloe, C. (2014) *Bananas, Beaches and Bases: Making Feminist Sense of International Politics.* University of California Press.

Netton, I. (ed.) (2008) *Encyclopedia of Islamic Civilization and Religion*. New York: Routledge.

Ravazi, S. and Miller, C. (1995) From WID to GAD: conceptual shifts in the women and development discourse. Occasional Paper 1. New York: United Nations Research Institute for Social Development.

UN Women (2012) Women entrepreneurship to reshape the economy in MENA through innovation, 17 October. New York: UN Women. Available at http://www.unwomen.org/en/news/stories/2012/10/wo men-entreprencurship-to-reshape-the-economy-in-mena-thr ough-innovation-high-level-panel-during-eu (accessed 5 May 2015).

UN Women (2013) *Regional Consultation for the Proposed General Recommendation on Women Human Rights in Situations of Conflict and Post Conflict Contexts*. Amman: UN Women. Available at http:// www.ohchr.org/Documents/HRBodies/CEDAW/Womenconflictsit uations/RegionalConsultationAmmanJan2013.pdf (accessed 30 July 2015).

UN Women (2015) *Summary: Arab Regional Synthesis Report on the Implementation of the Beijing Platform for Action Twenty Years Later*. New York: UN Women.

World Bank (2010) Middle East and North Africa: Women in the Workforce. Available at http://web.worldbank.org/WBSITRIES/MENAE XT/EXTMNAREGTOPVRED/0,,contentMDK:22497617~pagePK:34 004173~piPK:34003707~theSitePK:497110,00.html (accessed 1 May 2015).

World Bank (2011) *World Development Report 2012: Gender Equality and Development*. Washington, DC: World Bank.

World Bank (2013a) *Opening Doors: Gender Equality and Development in the Middle East and North Africa*. MENA Development Report. Washington, DC: World Bank.

World Bank (2013b) *Jordan Country Gender Assessment: Economic Participation, Agency and Access to Justice in Jordan*. Report ACS5158. Washington, DC: World Bank.

World Bank (2014) Ease of Doing Business Index. Available at http://da ta.worldbank.org/indicator/IC.BUS.EASE.XQ (accessed 1 May 2015).

World Economic Forum (2014) *The Global Gender Gap Report 2014.* Geneva: World Economic Forum.

Zuhayli, W. (1986) *Tafsir al-Muneer* [The Enlightened Exegesis], Volume 21–22. Beirut: Dar al-Fikr.

7 JIHAD AND POLITICAL CHANGE: A PERSPECTIVE BASED ON QURANIC SOURCES

M. A. Muqtedar Khan

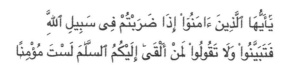

يَـٰٓأَيُّهَا ٱلَّذِينَ ءَامَنُوٓاْ إِذَا ضَرَبْتُمْ فِى سَبِيلِ ٱللَّهِ فَتَبَيَّنُواْ وَلَا تَقُولُواْ لِمَنْ أَلْقَىٰٓ إِلَيْكُمُ ٱلسَّلَـٰمَ لَسْتَ مُؤْمِنًا

O You who believe, when you go forth to fight in the cause of Allah, investigate, and do not tell someone who offers you peace, You are not a believer.

Quran 4:94

In the past few years, the Islamic Middle East has experienced a political roller coaster that gave the region a brief taste of democracy before authoritarianism was restored with an added dose of uncertainty, chaos and a steady erosion of the state as a viable political entity. While 2011 promised exhilarating change and democratisation, following a political moment often described as the Arab Spring (Ramadan 2012), 2013 and 2014 not only reversed the gains of 2011 but brought more war, more oppression and more violence to the region. Muslims have experienced and witnessed how change could be brought through peaceful means, as in Tunisia and Egypt, and they have also witnessed how violence and civil war can destroy states and unleash demons of sectarianism and terrorism as in Syria and Iraq.

In 2011, I argued that the emerging trend of political protests as witnessed so spectacularly in Tahrir Square, Cairo, would make violent extremist groups such as al-Qaida extinct, but history has proven me wrong with the emergence of Islamic State in Iraq and Syria (ISIS) (Muqtedar Khan 2011). The jihadi group has not only proven to be more cruel and extreme than even al-Qaida, it has also been more active. Where as al-Qaida merely attacked, ISIS captures and holds territory and has even declared an Islamic Caliphate. It is the failure of peaceful efforts to bring about political transformation in Syria without even minor changes as in Morocco and Jordan, that has led to the civil war and the subsequent rise of ISIS. This chapter, while inspired by these events, is, however, not about the region's geopolitics. Instead, it examines the theology of the use of force for political change in Islamic sources. It is about *jihad* and political change.[1]

The most pressing problem of the contemporary Islamic world is how to bring about fundamental political, social and economic restructuring while maintaining peace. The Muslim world cannot be allowed to degenerate into religious intolerance and it cannot exist under secular tyranny. People in most Muslim societies today are deprived of their basic rights, have little freedom of religion and scarce opportunities for economic development. A lot of resources are being wasted in wars, civil wars and in weapons accumulation and this environment undermines the stability that is necessary for a flourishing economy based on the rule of law and private property. The states in most Muslim countries seem to have a *raison d'être* independent of the interests of the people. Except in oil-rich Gulf states, where consent is bought through welfare and economic concessions, Muslim states, particularly in Asia and Africa, have very little to offer for their people. Some states, such as Syria and Egypt, even cause great misery for their own people. Given these dire conditions,

---

1   For a systematic study of jihad, see Afsaruddin (2013) and Muqtedar Khan (2004).

the absolute necessity of systemic change in the Muslim world has to be recognised (see Esposito and Muqtedar Khan 2000). While many of the problems in the Muslim and Arab world appear to be political and religious in nature, as people demand democracy and more freedom for religion in the public sphere, one cannot escape the reality of economic underdevelopment. The most stable states are either democracies (for example, Malaysia and Turkey) or monarchies (for example, Saudi Arabia and Qatar). However, it can be argued that the source of their stability is not regime type but rather economic development, as all those four countries have a reasonably high income and quality of life.[2]

Colonialism and post-colonialism

The countries of the Muslim world have yet to recover from the post-colonial moral crisis that they have all experienced (Mitchell 1991). Colonial domination precipitated a gradual but systematic erosion of the institutions of Muslim civil society. The decline of traditional institutions of justice, social welfare, education and social affiliations has left a huge moral vacuum. The end of the colonial era did not give Muslim societies any respite from the cultural and value invasion of the West. Indeed the new regimes, often led by ultra nationalists (such as Atatürk of Turkey and Nasser of Egypt), sought to rapidly transform or even Westernise the societies they inherited. They never gave themselves the opportunity to collect themselves and resuscitate the moral fabric of their societies, which had been ravaged by foreign domination. Once free from foreign intervention, these leaders rushed to emulate their former oppressors. Thus, after fighting foreign colonialism, the already debilitated Muslim society had to fight

---

2   See also Wilson (2012). Of course, it could also be argued that regime stability helps promote economic growth.

another war of independence, but this time against internal colonialism in pursuit of an authentic identity and society (Muqtedar Khan 1998). This second anti-colonial upsurge has come primarily through the resurgence of Islam, which in many ways is an effort to resuscitate and revive the authentic moral fabric of Muslim societies (Mansfield and Pelham 2013; Kabir Hassan and Lewis 2014).

Peace, non-violence and the difficulty of meaningful change

Enduring poverty, unemployment, absence of democracy and human rights and the persistence of authoritarian regimes in the Muslim Middle East has made the political status quo unviable (Muqtedar Khan 2007). That economic and political change is necessary in the Middle East is incontestable. The issue that public intellectuals, community leaders, political movements and parties and opinion formers must contemplate is whether this change can be engineered peacefully or whether it will have to be violent. Before we can reflect on any substantive issues regarding the impulse for change and the form this change will take, we must examine the idea of peace and non-violence itself. What is the intrinsic value of peace and non-violence? Are they to be valued in themselves to such an extent that the fear of violence and instability in the process of change compels us to defer change indefinitely?

The key challenge that newly democratised regimes in Egypt and Tunisia faced after the Arab Spring was the daunting task of bringing social equality and economic development to their population. In both Egypt and Tunisia, the Islamist governments sought to make symbolic gains without genuine material transformation and eventually failed. The Arab Spring was driven by economic despair and the search for dignity, not by a desire for political participation. Democracy was a means to realise those goals but, ultimately, the rebellions were driven by a desire for economic well-being. Political change without economic change will not solve the problems in Muslim societies and will simply lead to counter-revolutions (Muqtedar Khan 2013) and recurring violence (Amin 2013).

If we regard peace and non-violence as desirable values with *intrinsic* worth that carry an absolute priority over everything else, this inevitably leads to the politics of status quo. If existing authoritarian regimes and ruling coalitions are not willing to relinquish power, even in the face of popular opposition such as in Syria, then doing nothing other than maintaining peace and stability would become an effective defence of the status quo, however bad the status quo is or however much a ruling regime lacks legitimacy. However, the need for change should not be taken as a licence to resort to egregious violence that destroys the social fabric, historical monuments and any hope of reconciliation between different segments of the society.

If non-peaceful or violent means are sometimes to be used, then there must be clearly identifiable values, the intrinsic worth of which must be greater than that of peace. It is only when such values are identified that peace can be compromised in pursuit of these values, which are more precious than peace itself. I wonder how many would challenge my contention that justice, equality and freedom are more valuable than peace? I am not willing to give up my freedom, or allow myself to be treated as inferior or be treated unjustly, without a fight. Can we demand that people give up their rights, their freedoms and accept injustices in the interest of maintaining order?

I believe that we cannot. However, despite this, we can appeal to the oppressed and the downtrodden to give 'peaceful change' a chance. We can at least defend peace as an instrumental value even if we cannot defend peace as an inherent value worth more than all other values. Particularly in a region where change is necessary, the engineering of peaceful, gradual and systematic change will preclude violent and revolutionary transformations. We can develop a discourse based on Quranic principles of peace to advance Islamic ethical theories of international and inter-faith relations (Muqtedar Khan 1997).

Jihad for change

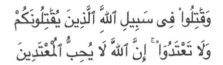

And fight in the Way of Allah those who fight you,
but transgress not the limits. Truly, Allah likes not the
transgressors.

Quran 2:190

The Quran offers a very sophisticated view of peace (Khan 2013). In many verses it promises the believer peace as a final reward for a righteous life (5:16). It also describes the house of Islam as the abode of peace (10:25). At the behest of the Quran, Muslims greet each other every time they meet, by wishing peace for each other (6:54). However, the Quran does not shy away from advocating military action in the face of persecution and religious intoler-ance. The strongest statement is in the chapter al-Baqarah (191): 'And slay them wherever you find them, and drive them out of the places from where they drove you out, for persecution is worse than slaughter.'

The presence of this verse in the Quran clearly precludes a complete prohibition of violence. The verse is important because, in spite of the enormous significance that the Quran attaches to peace and harmony, it is categorical in its assertion that persecu-tion is worse than killing. There is nothing allegorical in this verse, it is clear: 'persecution is worse than killing' (2:217). Elsewhere the Quran states: 'And fight them until persecution is no more' (8:39). The Quranic preference for struggle against persecution and its promise to reward those who struggle in the path of Allah (4:74) means that the only way violence can be eliminated from the Muslim world is by eliminating injustices and persecution. But the Quran also demands that violence cease as soon as persecution ceases. Thus it seeks to balance the absence of conflict with the absence of injustice. However, in order that there be peace, there must be change, and this change is not necessarily peaceful. But, perhaps we can minimise areas where violence is legitimised by the Quran.

In al-Baqarah, the Quran says: 'And fight them until persecution is no more, and religion is for Allah. But if they desist, then let there be no hostility except against wrongdoers' (2:193). This verse is interesting because it limits retaliation against all except those who are directly responsible for wrongdoing and also suggests that persecution could mean religious persecution. In other words, it is when the practice of Islam is prohibited that fighting persecution with violent means is justified. This could have implications for conflicts among Muslim states and between Muslim states and Islamic groups. Where Muslim citizens are allowed to practise their faith freely, as in Saudi Arabia, Pakistan and Iran, violence is not an option.

The Quran makes a profound pronouncement in al-Anfal: 'Tell those who disbelieve that if they cease (from persecution of believers) that which is past will be forgiven them' (8:38). This injunction further reduces the scope for violent response against persecution by granting an amnesty to those who stop persecution. One of the reasons that tyrannical regimes persist in the Muslim world is due to the fear of retaliation. Regimes are resisting change and democratisation for fear of being persecuted for past crimes by new regimes. A promise of a general amnesty for past deeds by potential challengers may create an atmosphere where existing regimes may permit gradual change.

Thus, philosophically, we may not be able to completely eliminate the revolutionary option for instituting change, but there is enough meat in the Quran to suggest that a violent response should be limited to egregious cases of religious persecution and repression. The Quran also makes a strong case for forgiveness and for peace as soon as hostilities are ceased. It also does not permit the use of force against those who do not use force.

Conflicts in the Islamic world

The Muslim world is today beset with political struggles which have the potential for violent conflict. At one level the Muslim world is still locked in an ideological, political and sometimes even violent struggle with states which are non-Muslim in character. At another level, Muslim states are involved in conflict against each other as well as in internal conflicts and civil wars. Even constitutional democracies such as Pakistan face both peaceful and violent challenges from within while also being involved in conflicts outside their borders.

In addition, there are problems of conflict between state and society, for example, in Syria and Egypt. This type of conflict has attracted the most attention because it pits Islamists against usually non-democratic but secular and sometimes pro-Western regimes. These conflicts inspire great fear in the West because most analysts in the West assume all potential Islamist states, if the Islamists succeed, will turn out to be like Iran – virulently anti-West and anti-Israel. Finally, we have the civil conflict between the secularists and the Islamists (Muqtedar Khan 2001).

The state is inevitably involved in this struggle as it is often pressed into the service of one or the other party as has happened in Turkey, Pakistan and Algeria. All these struggles have resulted in a great deal of violence, raising questions such as 'can Muslims resolve their differences peacefully?' and 'do they have a tradition for tolerance and the peaceful resolution of conflict?'

This leads to the specific question, which is a challenge to Muslims, of whether we can find some philosophical foundations for peaceful resolution of conflict over Muslim mores whose revival may help to introduce regimes that can facilitate peaceful conflict resolution and peaceful socio-political change. A search for answers to these questions will entail an analysis of Islamic sources for any injunctions relating to peace and an understanding of barriers to peaceful processes. The arguments below will be limited to Quranic sources given that the Quran alone remains an uncontested source of moral authority in almost all sections of the Muslim world.

The Quran and the way to peace

The value of peace is clear in the message of the Quran. It treats peace as the desired path in life as well as a value or reward for righteousness. In chapter al-Maidah, the Quran states that God guides all those who seek his pleasure to ways of peace and security (5:18). The same verse draws a profound parallel between the ways of peace and the movement from darkness to light, onto the straight path. There can be no doubt that this verse of Surat al-Maidah is positing the transition from *Jahiliyyah* to Islam, from darkness to enlightenment, from being misguided onto the *sirat al-mustaqeem* (the straight path) as a way to peace: 'Whereby Allah guides him who seeks His good pleasure unto paths of peace. He brings them out of darkness unto light by his will, and guides them unto a straight path' (Quran 5:16).

In the verse cited at the beginning of this chapter, the Quran describes Islam as the abode of peace (10:25). Indeed the word Islam, which means submission, is a derivative of the word *salam* meaning peace. Muslims greet each other by wishing or praying for peace for each other – as-salamu 'alaykum (may peace be upon you). This is not based on a tradition or a convention: it is a practice based on the injunctions of the Quran. The Quran states that the greeting of those who are righteous and who have been admitted to the heavens is 'Peace!' (14:23). It is quite amazing the degree to which Muslims have lost their self-awareness about being Muslim and its significance in terms of being bringers of peace. If they were to become more self-conscious about their faith and the elements of their faith that they practise, it would help to bring more social harmony and peace to the Muslim world.

Peace as an important goal is not limited to relations within the Muslim community. It is desired with other communities too. The Quran forbids Muslims from initiating aggression or causing fitna (mischief or rioting) on earth and exhorts them to make peace with their enemies if their enemies incline towards peace. For example:

- 'Wrong not humanity in their goods, and do not do evil or make mischief on earth' (26:183).
- 'Fight in the way of Allah against those who fight against you, but begin not hostilities. Lo! Allah loves not aggressors' (2:190).
- 'If they withdraw from you but fight you not, and (instead) send you (guarantees of) peace, then Allah has opened no way for you (to war against them)' (4:90).
- 'But if the enemy incline towards peace, you too should incline towards peace, and trust in God: for He is One that hears and knows (all things)' (8:61).

Verse (8:61) has direct contemporary relevance. One of the biggest hurdles to peace today is insecurity stemming from distrust of potential partners in peace. Parties demand guarantees of peace and impose preconditions for peace, which in themselves have become barriers to peace. But the Quran addresses these insecurities and advises Muslims to go ahead and make peace if the enemy shows even the slightest inclination to do so, with trust and faith in Allah who knows and hears everything. Clearly,

Allah supports those who make peace and they need not let uncertainties preclude the realisation of peace.

Conclusion

The Quran forbids Muslims from initiating or perpetuating violence except in self-defence and to fight persecution. Persecution is a complex phenomenon and the meaning of the term is often contingent on contemporary realities. But, broadly, it can be considered as a condition in which people are deprived of the freedom to practice their beliefs and their property, their land and their lives are constantly in jeopardy. The Quran is a strong advocate of peace, but it does permit Muslims to fight to protect their faith, freedom and lands and property.

But, in the interests of peace and to avoid the inevitable persecution and misery that comes with violence, Muslim scholars and intellectuals can argue that violence should be the last resort. They can demand of all agents of change that they pursue all avenues of peaceful change before they resort to revolutionary tactics. This brief discussion of the Quran is indicative of the value of peace for Muslims, both within the community and outside. However, the mere presence of divine injunctions for peace is not a guarantee of peace. The task of translating these Quranic principles into concrete reality remains one of the biggest challenges for Muslim scholars and Muslim intellectuals. The importance of this cannot be overstated. A peaceful society is a necessary precondition for a flourishing economy. If property is under threat and violence common, and if the ownership of resources is determined by violent conflict rather than through peaceful cooperation in a free economy based on private property and the rule of law, it is almost impossible to envisage a flourishing economic life. In the same way, a stable society requires that political power is transferred peacefully through largely democratic means.

References

Afsaruddin, A. (2013) *Striving in the Path of God: Jihad and Martyrdom in Islamic Thought*. Oxford University Press.

Amin, M., Assaad, R., al-Baharna, N., Derviş, K., Desai, R. M., Dhillon, N. S., Galal, A., Ghanem, H., Graham, C. and Kaufmann, D. (2012) *After the Spring: Economic Transitions in the Arab World*. Oxford University Press.

Esposito, J. L. and Muqtedar Khan, M. A. (2000) Religion and politics in the Middle East. In *Understanding the Contemporary Middle East* (ed. D. Gerner). Boulder, CO, and London: Lynne Rienner Publishers.

Kabir Hassan, M. and Lewis, M. K. (2014) Islam, the economy and economic life. In *Handbook on Islam and Economic Life*, Chapter 1.

Khan, M. W. (2013) *Islam and Peace*. New Delhi: Goodword Books.

Malik, A. and Awadallah, B. (2013) The economics of the Arab Spring. *World Development* 45: 296–313.

Mansfield, P. and Pelham, N. (2013) *A History of the Middle East*. London: Penguin Books.

Mitchell, T. (1991) *Colonizing Egypt*. University of California Press.

Muqtedar Khan, M. A. (1997) Islam as an ethical tradition of international relations. *Islam and Christian-Muslim Relations* 8(2): 177–92.

Muqtedar Khan, M. A. (1998) Constructing identity in 'glocal' politics. *American Journal of Islamic Social Sciences* 15(3): 81–106.

Muqtedar Khan M. A. (2001) The political philosophy of Islamic resurgence. *Cultural Dynamics* 13(2): 211–29.

Muqtedar Khan, M. A. (2004) *Jihad for Jerusalem: Identity and Strategy in International Relations*. New York: Greenwood Publishing Group.

Muqtedar Khan, M. A. (2007) *Debating Moderate Islam: The Geopolitics of Islam and the West*. Salt Lake City, UT: University of Utah Press.

Muqtedar Khan, M. A. (2011) View of the Arab Spring through a French window. *Huffington Post*, 21 October. (Available at http://www.huffing tonpost.com/muqtedar-khan/view-of-the-arab-spring-t_b_1023 068.html.)

Muqtedar Khan, M. A. (2014) Islam, democracy and Islamism after the counterrevolution in Egypt. *Middle East Policy* 21(1): 75–86.

Ramadan, T. (2012) *The Arab Awakening: Islam and the New Middle East.* Oxford University Press.

Wilson, R. (2012) *Economic Development in the Middle East.* Routledge.

8 ISLAM AND POLITICS TODAY: THE REASONS FOR THE RISE OF JIHADISM

Hasan Yücel Başdemir

The problem

Today, political unrest and violence dominate in the Islamic world. In almost every corner of the Middle East, governments are in power that do not allow basic rights to those who are in peaceful opposition. The search for a life of peace is thwarted either by bombs, unknown assassins and military coups, or by jihadi (Islamic militant) groups, and the destructive and aggressive attitudes of Islamaphobic secularists. Certain terrorist groups consider this an opportunity and are trying to realise their political objectives under the name 'Islamic State', justified by 'Sharia' (Islamic ecclesiastical law) and using violence as a tool. Outside the Islamic world, the majority of Muslims are integrated within the societies in which they live; however, some of them are experiencing problems of integration. In short, Muslims are facing serious social problems all over the world.

Of course, there is no single reason for these problems. The world conjuncture, the global economic situation, local factors, struggles between religious sects and the tension arising from a lack of strategy over oil and natural resources, all cause their problems. However, perhaps the overriding problem is that Muslim people cannot produce a way of living on which they can fully agree. The intelligentsia and academics cannot properly analyse what is going on or foresee the future because the problems are so intricate. There is no consensus around the meaning of Islamic political concepts.

There is, of course, much debate around Sharia. This concept has bad connotations in the Western world and also among secular Muslims. Though religious people praise Sharia, its meanings are different to different people. Most Muslims see Sharia as the dynamic reflection of Islam on everyday life that can change according to new situations. Jihadi groups, on the other hand, interpret Sharia as the unchangeable and unfailing laws of Allah on Earth. Uncertainty and violence provide propaganda for the radical and jihadi groups, and, for this reason, their supporters are increasing in number.

The adaptation of Muslim people to the world in which they live and also the promotion of peace in the Muslim world depend on the ability of Muslim people to agree to respect differences peacefully. Unfortunately, Islamic communities are unsuccessful in forming a conventional and agreeable political culture. Today, these problems are being discussed in every corner of the Islamic world.

In this chapter we will examine the modern political dispositions in the Muslim world in the context of the increasing power of jihadi movements, which have now become a major threat for the whole world. Whether Muslim or not, people who are under the pressure of violence and terror are curious about this: from where does the Islamic understanding of the jihadis stem? Jihadis claim that their beliefs are based on the Sharia, and this Sharia includes the facts that were stated by the Prophet Muhammad. They claim that there is only one single interpretation of the religion. This interpretation is for everyone.

The political uncertainties in the Islamic world have given rise to an increase in support for jihadis. From where do they obtain their support? Is it the message of Muhammad, or is it the sociological experiences people have undergone? To answer this question, it is necessary to glimpse into the history of the political experiences of the Muslim people.

We can divide this history into two different historical periods. The first is the political experience that starts with the holy voyage of the Prophet Muhammad to Medina (Yathrib) in the year 622 AD and continues until the early nineteenth century. The second period starts with colonisation in the nineteenth century and includes the political Islamic discourses produced against the secular dictatorships. Modern political attitudes have been born in this second period. These attitudes were moderate and agreeable in the beginning; however, they became controversial and exclusionist later on. Today, this exclusionist attitude has become a danger, both for the Muslim people and for the world.

The political experiences of the Prophet Muhammad and his followers

Before the Prophet Muhammad brought his Islamic message, the Arabs in the area called Hejaz lived in small city states, and did not have political unity. This region was surrounded by Byzantium to the north, Persia to the east, Abyssinia to the west, and the Yemen kingdom to the South. The Arabs were worried about attacks by these strong states and were afraid of losing the wealth that they had earned by commerce. In an era when the Arabs were in search of political unity, the Prophet Muhammad (571–632) brought the first revelations in 610. This new religion spread among the Arabian tribes within a very short time (around twenty years). As Islam was spreading among the Arabs, a political unity was being formed as well.

The Hijrah, the holy journey of the Prophet Muhammad from Mecca to Medina (Yathrib), occurred in the year 622, and the Muslim people started to form a state model. This process started with the Hijrah and gained speed with the conquest of Mecca in 630. As the message of Islam was spreading, a strong state was also emerging. After the year 630, Islam started to spread out of Hejaz as well, and the borders of the state were expanding.

Actually, the Prophet Muhammad did not claim any political leadership: he was a Prophet. However, the fact that there was not a strong state in Hejaz, and the expectations of the Arabs for political unity, made Muhammad a natural political leader. The political success of the Prophet Muhammad came before the religious successes. Before the Islamic message was completed, Muhammad proclaimed his political victory and established a strong state that could militarily defeat the Byzantium Empire and Persia in a very short time.

Muhammad did not promise a state to the Muslim people, and did not present a state model. He found himself as the political leader of the Muslims spontaneously while he was spreading his message. The religious and worldly authority was merged in the personality of Muhammad. The merger of these two authorities was not experienced before in the traditions of Abraham on whom Muhammad based his message. A similar situation was partly observed in the time of David and Solomon; however, the political power of Muhammad went far beyond theirs. Before the revelations ended, Muhammad took the authority of the state in his hands, and this authority was an effective tool for spreading the divine message. Actually, he did not have a political purpose; his sole aim was to convey the divine message to the whole of humanity. Muhammad, therefore, did not face an authority that prevented him from inviting people to Islam and this situation gave rise to a rapid spread of Islam. As the Islamic world was expanding, the practices of Muhammad became a political model for future rulers. This political model did not depend on the separation of the religion and politics. In the world of the seventh century AD, there was not a civil state in today's sense, and nor was there such an expectation.

Muhammad took political decisions because he was also the head of the state. What kind of route did he follow while he was taking these decisions? The word 'state' did not exist in the divine message, and an original state model or a political organisational form was not suggested. Muhammad made use of the general principles set forth by the divine message about social life. However, for most of the time, he did not find it unfavourable to take many practices that existed in the traditions of idolater Arabs so long they were not contrary to the divine message (Fazlurrahman 1995: 9).

The death of Muhammad started the political debates that later gave rise to two big religious sects (Shiite and Sunni). The followers of these debates took the political practices of Muhammad as the starting point. However, they did not accept his practices as unchangeable and added many new practices to them. The first political practice after the death of Muhammad was the Caliphate. The Caliphate involves somebody taking leadership of Muslims in the name of the Prophet to run religious and worldly affairs (Ebu'l Hasan el-Maverdi 1994: 29): this person is called the 'Caliph'. Muhammad did not propose such an institution and did not appoint a Caliph. After his death, Abu Bakr became the Caliph after elections. Before he died, Abu Bakr appointed Omar as the next Caliph. Omar gave the right of electing the Caliph after him to a strategic commission consisting of six people. This commission determined the Caliphate of Othman with an election process. Ali then became Caliph elected by the majority of Muslims like the first Caliph Abu Bakr. After Ali, the Caliphate was transferred to the Umayyad dynasty. With the Umayyads, the Caliphate was merged with the sultanate, and was transferred down the family line from father to son. After one century, the Abbasids followed the Umayyads. The Caliphate was a rational institution that emerged as a result of the needs of the Muslim people for earthly leadership and was not proposed by the Prophet.

The political structures that started with the Prophet Muhammad and continued with the 'Era of Four Caliphs' continued with the sultanates of Umayyads and Abbasids. However, this system took different forms according to the needs of the Islamic world throughout history. For example, the Ottoman Sultans established a religious authority called 'Sheik al-Islam' to make decisions (fatwas) on religious issues. The development of this state model continued until the seventeenth century, when the Ottoman state started to decline. The model was not a religious necessity; it developed as a result of human necessities.

Louise Massignon defined the Muslim state that emerged over this period as a 'secular and egalitarian theocracy' (Gardet 1977: 74). This definition shows that it is not possible to understand the political experience of Muslim people using the terminology of modern politics. When viewed from today's perspective, the Muslim state is theocratic in some ways and secular in other ways.

Characteristics of the early period state model

Al-Mawardi (974–1058), in his book *Al-Ahkam al-Sultania w'al-Wilayat al-Diniyya*, describes the characteristics of the state model that tended to govern Muslim peoples. Al-Mawardi claims that the Caliphs did not take their political power from Allah, and that they were elected or appointed. He makes a list of the duties of a Caliph. These duties are: protecting the religion; protecting the lives and property of the people; adjudicating disputes; setting penalties and applying them for the purpose of protecting the rights of the peoples; applying the orders and prohibitions set by Allah; and conducting the necessary work to prove that Islam is superior to other religions. In addition, the Caliph is responsible for preparing for battle against those who want to harm the Muslim people.

In Al-Mawardi's books, we can find the characteristics of the early period state model. Acting in accordance with the Muslim religion, spreading and protecting it are the duties of the state. There has not been a distinction between the religion and politics in the historical and political experience of Muslims. The heads of states represented the highest religious and worldly authority, with the title Caliph (Zaman 1997: 208). For this reason, the Muslim state was not a secular state. However, it is also hard to claim that it was a full theocracy, because the Caliph, although he was the worldly and religious leader, was not a person who had spiritual properties. His decisions were not binding in terms of religion; they were only examples. The heads of states did not have spiritual superiority over other Muslims, and did not rule the country in the name of Allah. Moreover, the Caliph had the authority to make the laws of the country only as long as they were not contrary to the laws and orders of Allah.

Also important were the 'dhimmis'. Dhimmis were people who were not Muslims but who accepted Muslim political authority. They were restricted by various laws and, unlike Muslims, paid an extra tax called the 'poll tax' (jizya). In return, they were exempt from military service and some other responsibilities. The state ensured the safety of their properties and their lives. This practice was based on the verses of the Quran (al-Mumtahanah 60:9): 'Allah does not prohibit you from making good deeds and behaving in justice to those who do not make war with you'; and on the agreements of the Prophet Muhammad with the Jews and Christians in Medina. The dhimmis and Muslims had equal commercial rights. They were allowed to establish a worldly and religious authority that regulated their internal and external affairs in the society in which they lived. Based on these practices, we can conclude that multiple legal systems were allowed in Muslim countries. The dhimmis were tried according to their own legal systems if they demanded it.[1]

The existence of multiple legal systems was an important part of Muslim political life. This was apparent from the time of the Prophet Muhammad until the collapse of the Ottoman state. In addition, the legal system of the Muslim people was divided into two subclasses: ecclesiastical law and customary law. The

---

1   Ibn Qayyim al-Cavziyya, *Ahkamu Ahli'd-Dhimme* [The Law of Dhimmes].

ecclesiastical law consisted of laws based on interpretations of the Quran and Sunna. The customary law consisted of the laws that were needed and made by the rulers. The Ottoman state developed this double system and made it more systematic.

Politics as part of Sharia

The development of the historical Muslim state model did not ensure that politics and ethics were developed independently from religion. Books written on ethics and politics were not favoured by society or its rulers. For this reason, topics such as government and law in Islam were considered under the title of disciplines such as Fiqh (Islamic jurisprudence) and Kalam (Islamic theology) in classical sources. As a result of this, the political terms and approaches that emerged were accepted as part of Islamic belief.

Islamic belief is traditionally divided into four sections.

- Belief: this includes the belief principles such as believing in Allah, the Prophets, holy books and the hereafter.
- Worshipping, including prayers, fasting and zakat (Islamic charity).
- 'Muamelat' (relations/proceedings), which relates to commerce, inheritance, marriage, divorce and other similar legal issues. The issues about governing the state are also part of this area.
- Punishments or penalties (*ukubat*), which refer to the legal system of punishment.

These four elements are expressed in the word 'Sharia'. The word Sharia means road, method and custom. When the word Sharia is mentioned, usually the Islamic state order is understood. But, the state order constitutes a very small part of Sharia. Sharia is a set of rules that is intended to organise the individual, social, religious and worldly lives and affairs of Muslims. These rules are based on the Quran and Sunna that are accepted as the main sources of Islam. The Quran is the holy book of Allah revealed to the Prophet Muhammad. The Sunna is the words and deeds of the Prophet Muhammad. Sunna is the way the Quran is applied in practice by the Prophet Muhammad.

The Quran and Sunna are the basic sources of Islam. The authority of these cannot be questioned. However, they are open to interpretation and adaptation to new conditions. As the founder of the religious sect of Hanafites, Abu Hanifa (699–767), said: 'Interpreting the events does not make a man go astray unless the revelations from Allah are denied'. The interpretations of the Quran and Sunna that are designed to make the main sources of the religion understood and adaptable to new conditions constitute Sharia. The religion is not questioned and is stable; however, Sharia is dynamic and changeable. Indeed, different interpretations constitute the bases of the various religious sects. For this reason, there is not a single code of Sharia on which all Muslims fully agree. However, except for some disagreements in Shiite and Sunni religious sects, the many different rules of Sharia are not in conflict with each other: they are adapted to different times, places and cultures.

The belief and worshipping parts in Sharia are similar in different religious sects. However, there are many differences in Muamelat. The reason for this is that relations and proceedings are the part of Sharia in which interpretations are most needed. These interpretations are no mere opinion, however. There are certain methods by which they are derived, for example analogy, agreement of the Islamic society (ijama'), the stating of judicial opinion (ijtihad) and personal interpretation. Agreement of the Islamic society (ijama') and the stating of judicial opinion (ijtihad) are the most used methods in the area of relations. However, there are 'free legal areas' (ibaha) in classical Islamic jurisprudence (fıqh) which allow the taking of decisions without referring to the basic sources of the religion. The majority of the Sharia and politics is considered to be in the ibaha area.

There are many approaches to understanding Sharia, its nature and application. Shatibi from Andalucía (1320–88) claimed that Sharia is organised for the good of human beings both in the world and in the life hereafter. According to him, Sharia exists to protect innate rights. This is the purpose of Allah in sending the religion. In Shatibi's opinion, the real purpose of Sharia is protecting the five basic rights:

- Protecting the religion (freedom of religion).
- Protecting the human soul (human life or right to life).
- Protecting family life, including continuity from one generation to the next.
- Protecting property.
- Protecting thought (Ṣatibi 1990: 9, 24, 46) (this can be loosely interpreted as freedom to hold opinions and freedom of conscience).

These are called 'the purposes of Sharia' or, in Arabic, 'Maqasid al-Sharia'.

In the traditional Sunni belief system, there are two points of view about Sharia: Ahl al-Ra'y (the Exegetes) and Ahl al-Hadith (the Scripturists). Ahl al-Ra'y accept the realm of legal freedom in a broad sense and claim that the Holy Scriptures can be continually interpreted according to new conditions. As Shatibi said, the orders that are sent by Allah and mental and scientific truths are never in conflict. If there appears to be such a conflict, it is necessary that it is removed through interpretation. The widest religious sects of the Islamic world, Hanafites, al-Maturidi, Mu'tazilites and Maliki take this approach. Ahl al-Hadith (the Scripturists), on the other hand, deny the possibility of interpretation of the holy books and the legal freedom when it comes to the Sharia. According to them, everything that is needed is in the Holy Scriptures. Even if it is in conflict with science and mental truths, everything written in the fundamental scriptures is literally true and not open to interpretation. This attitude is generally called 'Salafiyya' and is mostly observed in the Hanbali religious sect. However, whether people adopt this position does not necessarily depend on whether they are members of a particular sect; such religious attitudes usually stem from personal preferences.

Modern jihadi movements find supporters from all religious sects and adopt the attitude of Ahl al-Hadith regarding the holy books. Ahl al-Hadith consider the religion and Sharia identical, and, for this reason, consider Sharia as a set of unchanging rules.

Colonisation and the birth of modern Islamic movements

Political experience in the last two centuries has gone through several periods from moderate political attitudes towards radical and violent ones. The period of colonisation continued until the 1940s and 1950s. This period caused two perspectives to emerge: the Islamist perspective and the reformist perspective. Both have accommodated modernist, moderate political attitudes, as well as anti-Western attitudes to some extent. Nevertheless, the approach of many Islamists has been to 'look back to the essence', ignoring traditional Islamic values (with the exception of the Quran and Sunna) and rejecting Muslims' historical experience. Reformists have defended Western values to the Muslim world. Both groups have avoided extremism. Islamists mostly defended a link between the Quran and the political sphere, not to promote violent discourse, but to promote pluralism, democracy and other modern Western values. Some Islamists even claimed that some secular political processes are acceptable even if not all are.

Reformists reject going 'back to basics' and linking the Quran to the political sphere. They remain secular in the field of politics, economics, etc. They defend Western values as they are. We can attribute 'modernism' to both groups, but not reformism.

There are at least two reasons for the change in attitude towards the use of violence in the political process in the last two centuries. Firstly, there have been the secular dictatorships that have restricted human rights. Secondly, there has been the development of new thinking as described above. The events of the last few decades did not increase the will to use violence, but did increase the social base of pro-violence groups. Although jihadism takes the approach of Ahl al-Hadith in terms of its belief system, it is a modern phenomenon. It was the political experience of Muslims in the last two centuries that made jihadism emerge. Islamic movements in the colonisation period were generally moderate. However, after the replacement of colonisation by secular dictatorships, first the fundamentalist, then the jihadi movements gained power. Having said that, it is still a fact that the historical conditions which helped lay the ground for jihadism started via the colonisation of the Muslim world by European states.

The traditional state model of Muslims was based on a strong leader who held religious and worldly authority. Through colonisation, Muslims lost the political power they had been holding for centuries and the traditional state model became inoperative.

This situation left most of the Muslim peoples behind the Europeans, who were more skilful in terms of political organisation. Colonisation gave rise to great political and attitudinal changes in the Muslim world. In the period that started in 622 AD, with the holy voyage of the Prophet Muhammad and his friends from Mecca to Medina, and continued until the invasion of Egypt by Napoleon in 1798, Muslims often held economic, scientific and political superiority over other religions and nations. The invasion of Egypt and the start of the British East India Company's governing role in India were the first indicators of the superiority of the Western world over Muslims. This superiority was then converted into colonisation and caused great disappointment. This disappointment urged Muslim scholars to set off on new quests.

Since the problem was political, it was political interpretations of Islam that came to the fore. A political science that was independent of religion did not develop and the new ideas that did develop were centred on religion. At first, the problem was stated along the following lines: 'Muslims have lagged behind. The reason for this is that they misinterpreted the religion and strayed away from the true religion. If we understand the religion truly, and apply it in our lives, we will be saved from disgrace and from being exploited.' In this context, the first political Islamic interpretations showed 'back to basics' and 'reform' characteristics.

Jamal al-Din al-Afghani (1838–97) from India was the founder of 'back to basics' theology. He was followed by Muhammad Abduh (1849–1905), Namık Kemal (1840–88), Rashid Rida (1865–1935), Muhammad Iqbal (1877–1938) and Musa Jarullah Bigiev (1873–1949), who were all Islamic modernists.

The ideas of 'revival' (ihya) and 'renewal' (tajdeed) lie at the heart of the 'back to basics' concept. According to these ideas, the reason for the then-current situation of Muslims was that they believed that Islamic thought was fixed. Afghani stated in his newspaper *al-Urwah al-Wuthqa* (*The Great Struggle for Salvation*), cowritten with Muhammad Abduh, which was an inspiration for the Islamic movements, that Muslims were left behind and exploited because they had moved away from the Quran and the Sunna (Ramadan 2005: 70).

Iqbal took a different view. According to him, the problem was the transition of Islamic thought into a 'hereafterism' and towards irrationality after its fifth century (Iqbal 2013: 215). This meant that the revival of Islamic thought should be based on leaving the traditional Quran and Sunna interpretations, and reinterpreting the main sources.

This first political Islamic movement, pioneered ideologically by Afghani, is known as Pan-Islamism. Pan-Islamism is not, contrary to popular belief, a jihadi movement. It is an intellectual and tolerant movement. It is intellectual, because Pan-Islamists believe that salvation does not come from battle, but from knowledge. It is tolerant because Pan-Islamists claim that Western values should be adapted to the Islamic world after they are checked and verified by the Quran. A hostile attitude towards the Western world is not observed in Islamist thought. Their motto can be summed up in this way: 'Take the science and technique of the West, but do not take its religion and culture'. So, it is faithful to the sacred texts in relation to their role in religion and culture. The biggest political aim of Afghani and his followers was the establishment of an Islamic Union and an Islamic Council as a form of consultation body for Islamic countries. The Ottoman State adopted Pan-Islamism as state policy over the years 1876–1923, when it was about to collapse.

Pan-Islamists were moderate towards secular values such as democracy and human rights. The Islamic Council was used as the manifestation of the term 'democracy' in the Muslim world by modernists such as Jamal al-Din al-Afghani and Muhammad Abduh. Pan-Islamists always claimed values that came from the tradition of European liberal politics. Hasan al-Banna (1906–49), who founded the Muslim Brotherhood organisation in Egypt, Rached Ghannouchi (1941–), who was the leader of the An-Nahda in Tunisia, and the Nationalistic Vision Movement led by Necmettin Erbakan (1926–2011) in Turkey based their political views on a democratic discourse. Pan-Islamists never saw armed struggle and violence as a method for seeking rights.

The general attitude of the Pan-Islamists has been that Muslims must overcome their problems with knowledge, work, sincerity and good moral values. However, some Pan-Islamists deny the religion–state separation, and defend a democracy, the basic principles of which are defined according to the main Islamic sources. Other modern Pan-Islamists, on the other hand, strongly defend political secularism. Although Erbakan and Ghannouchi opposed a form of secularism that held religious people away from the political life, they did consider the idea of separating politics from religion and ideology, thus secularising the state.

Another important political movement in the colonisation period was that of reformism. The emergence of reformism dates from around the same time as the emergence of Pan-Islamism. Reformism tries to make Islamic values and practices of modern life conform to each other and it proclaims democracy and political secularism. Reformists claim that religion and politics should be separated completely from each other and suggest that Muslims should take the political values and the science of the West as they are. According to reformists, the Quran and Sunna do not include judgements about politics: that should be left to the prudent judgements of human persons. The pioneer of this approach is Sir Sayyid Ahmad Khan from India.

Sayyid Ahmad Khan (1817–98) claimed that the current interpretation of Islam was against the development of science and art and that this was the reason for the Muslim world being left behind. He tried to adapt the natural religious approaches in the Western world (in the Age of Enlightenment) to Islam. Ahmad Khan influenced 'Ali 'Abd al-Raziq (1888–1966) in Egypt. 'Abd al-Raziq, in his book *Al-Islam wa Usul Al-Hukm*, states that Islamic Sharia is only spiritual and does not have laws and regulations for politics and for worldly matters. He argues that these issues are left to human judgement. According to 'Abd al-Raziq, Islam has left the worldly and political problems to the initiative of believers. The regulations about social life change in every period, and it is wrong to consider the practices in particular periods as the basis of Islam (Abdurrazık 1995: 42).

There has been lively discussion of the relationship between Islam and politics since the nineteenth century as a result of the trauma of colonisation. The religious-centred political discourses that started with Islamists as 'back to basics', 'renewal' and 'revival' theologies turned into the resistance theology, which was pitted against the secular dictatorships in the second half of the twentieth century.

From Pan-Islamism to jihadism

The jihadi movements became political actors in the Muslim world in the mid-twentieth century, originating from Pan-Islamic movements. However, there are many differences between Pan-Islamists and jihadis in terms of political attitudes and their views about religion and life. The emergence of revolutionary movements that favoured violence dates back to the 1940s. Two factors gave rise to these movements. The first was dictators obtaining power and torturing their peoples. The second was the wars in the Muslim world. The Arab–Israeli war that started after 1948, Israel's policies in relation to Palestine, the 1967 six-day war, the invasion of Afghanistan by the Soviet Union in 1979, the Bosnian War (1992–95) and the war in Chechnya (1994–96) – all of these strengthened jihadi movements.

The roots of jihadism and its birth

There has been a constant debate about how to describe the irreconcilable religious and political attitudes that have favoured violence in the Muslim world. They are given names such as 'radical Islamists', 'salafiyya', 'fundamentalists',[2] etc. However, jihadis describe themselves as 'mujahideen': those who fight a holy battle against people who do not believe in Islam. Jihadism, in this sense, corresponds to 'Islamic fundamentalism' within the political sphere.

---

2   Editorial note: The most commonly used phrase in the UK, certainly among government ministers, seems to be 'extremist'. This description is about as unhelpful as it gets. A group can take an extreme position on tolerance in relation to social issues (for example, the prime minister David Cameron); one could be extreme when it came to pacifism; there are many religious adherents (Mormons, Catholics, Strict Baptists, and, I am sure, many Muslims) who are extreme in their devotion, but they are in no sense violent or apologists for violence.

Jihad, as a word, means working and struggling. In the religious literature, jihad means that persons should work with all their strength, life, property and with language to make the name of Allah praised. Jihadism, on the other hand, has come to be the name of the attitude that emerged in mid-twentieth century in the Muslim world as a violent political struggle. Jihad, in classical Islamic literature, is the struggle of a person to live the religion, and to make it widespread. The self-struggle of a Muslim for being a helpful man of good moral values is also accepted as jihad: the Prophet Muhammad called this the 'Great Jihad'. Jihadis believe that they are already good people, and define jihad as giving battle against the non-believers in the name of Allah. They claim that they base their violent struggles on the principles of Islam and, for this reason, they emphasise certain concepts in the traditional religious understanding, and form a political discourse based on active struggle.

The jihadis give special meanings to religious concepts that are in accordance with their purposes and attitudes. They interpret the words in a way that allows them to give a religious justification for violence. Sharia and jihad are the most common words in this sense. These are followed by Caliph, dhimmi, Home of Islam (Dar al-Islam) and Home of War (Dar al-Harb).

Sharia, as stated above, is the side of the religion that is adjusted to the practicalities of life. However, the jihadis interpret Sharia as a destructive Islamic ideology that shows hostile attitudes towards different lifestyles. It should be noted that this is not an interpretation that is common in the Muslim world, but it is becoming more widespread both among Muslims who live in Western countries and among those who live in the Muslim world. Muslims who adopt the jihadi Islamic interpretation stay away from the society in which they live and close off channels of communication. They form religious safe houses and alternative lifestyles in the areas in which they live. They explain this lifestyle using the *jahiliyya* (ignorance) principle, arguing that those who do not live the religion as they do are either secular Muslims or non-believers and that they are 'ignorant' people who do not accept the sovereignty of Allah. In turn, they argue that they should stay away from others to protect themselves from this jahiliyya. According to the jihadis, Muslim people need political unity, and achieving it is a religious duty. For this, the caliphate must be revived. Jihadis claim that everybody except the dhimmis who beg pardon must be killed. They base their beliefs on the verse of the Quran in the Tawbah Surah: 'Kill the non-believers where you find them' (at-Tawbah 9:4–5). However, these verses were revealed in wartime conditions. There are many verses in the Quran stating that Muslim people must act in a good way to those who are not Muslims; they must act in justice even to those towards whom they feel anger (al-Maidah 5:8; al-Mumtahanah 60:9; 'Ali 'Imran 3:113). Jihadis respond by claiming that the advice to behave in a good way towards non-believers in these verses is 'overridden' by other verses. For example, the verse 'Kill the non-believers where you find them' overrides verses such as 'Muslim people must act in a good way towards those who are not Muslims'. They interpret Quranic verses as implying that a permanent state of war against non-Muslims is desirable. Jihadis exploit a particular methodology of interpretation to legitimise their violence.

The jihadis have three political principles:

1. Allah is the sole authority that can judge on any subject. Judgement belongs solely to Allah (*La Hukma Illa Lillah*).
2. Those who commit great sins are banished from the religion, and those who are banished from the religion should be killed.
3. War and riots against a cruel head of state are religious duties.

In fact, these three principles were defended by the 'Outers' who declared that the Caliph, Ali, was a heretic because he made an agreement with Muawiyah, the governor of Damascus, and killed him. Jihadis adopt the religious-political attitude of this first, uncompromising, pro-violence group in Islamic history. It is possible to divide jihadis into two groups, which could be described as 'theoretical' and 'practical'. Jihadism first emerged as a theoretical movement in the 1950s. Although there was resistance, violent actions were few and far between. However, the problem of Palestine, and the wars in Afghanistan, Bosnia and Chechnya, gave rise to the jihadis who had the ability and willingness to act. The mujahideen who gave battle against the Soviet invasion in Afghanistan began to fight in Bosnia after the war in Afghanistan was over. They then joined the Chechen war after the Bosnian war. Thus, there emerged a group who considered themselves to be holy warriors in the Muslim world, and who adopted war as their principal occupation. However, the jihadis did not only wage war in the frontiers, but also started to act violently against innocent civilians. The assault of al-Qaida on the Twin Towers in New York on 11 September 2001; the three bombings in Istanbul in 2003; and the terrorist attacks in Madrid in 2004 and in London in 2005 showed that practical jihadism was more than just a theoretical concept.

Jihadis came to believe that anywhere not ruled by the laws of Allah was a 'home of war' and that waging battle in such places was a religious duty.

The pioneers of the idea of jihadism

The emergence of this form of jihadism dates back to the mid-twentieth century when colonisation was replaced by dictatorships. The first jihadi discourses that emerged as opposition to the bad practices of dictators were in the form of political opposition. However, when such political opposition was faced with government power using violence and murder, the back-to-basics and renewal beliefs were replaced by the idea of resistance.

The basic thesis of the jihadis was that dictators proclaimed their own sovereignty after they ended the sovereignty of Allah. By doing so, they made the people their servants rather than the servants of Allah. The reason for the bad things that were happening to the people under these regimes was that the people were obeying these 'pharaohs' and tyrants.

Thus, they likened the dictators to the pharaohs who tortured the prophet Moses and Joseph, son of Jacob, in Egypt. It was argued that, when these pharaohs lost their political power, the sovereignty of Allah would be re-established and Muslims would be freed. Abul Ala Maududi (1903–79) and Sayyid Qutb (1906–66) became the most important intellectual pioneers of jihadism. According to Maududi and Qutb, secularism and democracy were 'the tools for intellectual colonisation that were imposed after the actual colonisation by the West in the Islamic world' (Qutb 1990: 114). They opposed political values such as democracy, pluralism, religious tolerance, protection of peace, freedom of expression and the separation of religion and the state because they were Western norms. Maududi and Qutb regarded secular dictators as Trojan horses sent to the Muslim world. The sole political sovereignty belongs to Allah (Qutb 1997). They worried about almost every thought that came from the outer world, and claimed that Muslims did not need anything from 'heretic Westerners'. For this reason, jihadism was based on protecting society, having society become more turned in upon itself and struggle.

The concept of 'the sovereignty of Allah' forms the basis of Maududi's political project. This has many implications: only Allah manages human persons; He is the superior lawmaker; man cannot make laws; we can neither make decisions about ourselves, nor can anybody else make decisions about us; nobody can force anyone else to obey them; rule and authority belong solely to Allah; the sole ruler on earth is Allah; the body that directs the sovereignty of Allah on earth is the Islamic Council; even the Islamic

Council that is formed of Muslim scholars cannot make laws – it only applies the Sharia (Milton-Edwards 2005: 26).

Maududi saw the holy battle, the jihad, as a revolutionary struggle for the good of all humanity. He argued that, just as the Prophet Muhammad struggled with the jahiliyya, today, Muslims should struggle with the jahiliyya (the ignorance) both in their own societies and in the West.

Maududi became a great source of inspiration for the fundamentalists in the Islamic world. His book *Four Terms According to the Quran* came to be described as the 'handbook of the resistance'. Sayyid Qutb, who was a socialist in his youth, was influenced by Maududi. He was imprisoned because of his beliefs and witnessed the violence used against the Islamists by the Nasser regime in the prisons of Egypt. This affected him profoundly, and he defended ideas that were more radical than Maududi. The books of Maududi and Sayyid Qutb became major works that formed a resistance theology based on the Quran in the Islamic world. For this reason, Maududi and Qutb may be regarded as the founders of jihadism with their resistance discourses (Armstrong 2000: 262).

Living out Islam in a free society

Jihadism emerged as a reaction against the social and political problems in the Muslim world in the last two centuries, and became stronger with the various wars and incidents of civil unrest. The religious-political discourses that started during the period of colonisation were converted into a resistance theology against secular dictatorships from the second half of the twentieth century. In the beginning, jihadism was an opposition discourse. However, later it was converted into actions that included violence.

Jihadis put Sharia at the central point of their political discourses, and consider the Sharia, politics and the state as a single whole that cannot be separated. They regard living the religion in a civil state order as blasphemy (*kufr*) and ignorance (jahiliyya). They believe it is necessary to abolish the 'blasphemy state' and establish the sovereignty of Allah under which they should live the religion. However, in the traditional Islamic state model, and in both the Shiite and Sunni traditions, there has not been an identity established between the legal system and the state. The historical state experience of the Muslim people allowed multiple legal systems. Also, the Muslim intelligentsia came to understand that traditional political experiences and Islamic sciences such as fiqh (Islamic jurisprudence) and kalam (Islamic theology) cannot find solutions for today's problems. For these reasons, sanctifying the historical experiences, carrying them up to today's world, and accepting them as unchangeable and unfailing, is futile.

Jihadi actions and discourses are not based on the main sources (the Quran and Sunna) as jihadis claim. On the contrary, jihadism is a phenomenon that emerged in the last few centuries and is an attitude held by people who cannot adapt themselves to the world they live in. The fact that some Muslim people who emigrate to Western countries adopt a religious form that is introverted and isolated from their neighbours is an indicator of this. Many Muslim peoples in the Muslim world, however, accept living under a state order that is civil and just and does not discriminate. Such Muslim peoples watch the pessimistic, uncompromising and violent actions of the jihadis in astonishment. The actions of ISIS are perceived in a similar way by an Anglican from England as by a Sunni Muslim in Turkey.

Muslim people should stop searching the past for solutions to political and social problems. They should solve their problems from an Islamic perspective that is appropriate for the realities of the world they live in. Muslim people must answer this question clearly: in what kind of a society do Muslim people want to live? Do they want to live in an Islamic state in which religious sects and different religious lifestyles are in conflict, or in a civil state in which the state is just and does not discriminate based on people's beliefs? Currently, there is no peace and stability in states that claim to be Islamic. And Muslim people are not free at all. The best choice before Muslims is to follow their religious beliefs freely in a civil state. Muslim people are suspicious of the civil state since it does not have a place in the historical experience of Islam: but, neither does an Islamic state.

The fact that the military coup in Egypt on 3 July 2013 was realised with the support of secularists and jihadis has shaken the belief of mild and optimistic religious people in democratic values. But, there is not a realistic option other than democracy. Muslim people need a society in which they can live freely not bound by the pessimistic, exclusionist and violent attitudes of jihadism. Neither discourses that bind Islam to violence, nor Islamophobia or military coups will prevent Muslim people from addressing their problems in a wise manner. The values of an open society await Muslim people.

References

Abdurrazık, A. (1995) *İslam'da İktidarın Temelleri* [*Bases of Government in Islam*] (translated by Ö. R. Doğrul). İstanbul: Birleşik Yayınları.

Armstrong, K. (2000) *The Battle for God*. New York: Knopf Press.

el-Maverdi, E. H. (1994) *el-Ahkamu's-Sultaniyye* [*Rules of Governance*] (translated by A. Şafak). İstanbul: Bedir Yayınevi.

Fazlurrahman (1995) İslam ve Siyasi Aksiyon: Siyaset Dinin Hizmetinde. *İslam'da Siyaset Düşüncesi* (translated by K. Güleçyüz). İstanbul: İnsan Yayınları.

Gardet, L. (1977) *Les Hommes de l'Islam: Approche des Mentalités*. Paris: Librairie Hachette.

Iqbal, M. (2013) *İslam'da Dini Düşüncenin Yeniden İnşası* [*The Restoration of Religious Thought in Islam*] (translated by R. Acar). İstanbul: Timaş Yayınları.

Milton-Edwards, B. (2005) *Islamic Fundamentalism Since 1945*. London: Routledge Press.

Qutb, S. (1990) *Ma'raka al-Islam wa al-Ra'smaliyya*. Cairo: Dar al-Shuruq.

Qutb, S. (1997) *Yoldaki İşaretler* [*Signposts on the Road*] (translated by S. Karataş). İstanbul: Dünya Yayınları.

Ramadan, T. (2005) *İslamî Yenilenmenin Kökenleri: Afgani'den el-Benna'ya Kadar İslam Islahatçılığı* (translated by A. Meral). İstanbul: Anka Yayınları.

Şatibi (1990) *el-Muvafakat fi Usuli'ş-Şeria*, Volume II (translated by M. Erdoğan). İstanbul: İz Yayıncılık.

Zaman, Q. (1997) *Religion and Politics under the Early Abbasids: The Emergence of the Proto-Sunni Elite*. New York: Brill.

9 ISLAM AND A FREE-MARKET ECONOMY: ARE THEY COMPATIBLE?

Hicham El Moussaoui

Deriving the Islamic attitude towards the economy is challenging since Islam as a religion is the aggregation of various texts, beliefs, views and practices and the economy as such is not the main focus. One gets further confused when the task is to examine the Islamic standpoint in relation to capitalism, socialism, free markets or a command economy as these are modern concepts that are meant to explain perceived economic reality. As such, there is always the potential pitfall of succumbing to extrapolations, anachronisms and hasty generalisations when comparing Islam with these concepts, which themselves do not have commonly agreed meanings. Bearing these caveats in mind, the following three points will be addressed in this chapter. Is Islam compatible with a free-market economy? If so, why are Arab economies so far from free-market principles? Finally, how can these principles be restored?

The foundations of Islam and a free-market economy are not incompatible

Islam has often been presented as incompatible with a free-market economy because of a socialist interpretation of certain Quranic verses (for example, in relation to issues such as collective ownership, the collectivisation of wealth, the prohibition of usury or interest and the rejection of conventional finance). However, such socialist interpretations are contradicted not only by several verses of the Quran and by the practices of the Prophet Muhammad, but also by the experience of Muslims, at least during the first age of Islam.

In this section, the compatibility between Islam and a free-market economy will be analysed through three pillars: free choice and the profit motive; the rule of law and contract; and competition.

Free choice and the profit motive

Islam teaches that we human persons are God's Caliph (the stewards of his creation). We cannot fulfil this charge without the liberty to choose good over evil of our own free will. Thus, the Quran says (2:256): 'Let there be no compulsion in religion'. Although Islam understands the fact that families and communities serve important functions and Islam requires the individual to fulfil his obligations to those institutions, the Quran seeks to reform society by reforming the individual. It appeals to morality and not to coercion, which it expressly prohibits.

Freedom to choose under the law and without coercion does not only concern issues that might be said to pertain to the life hereafter (that is, moral activities), but also the worldly life (commercial activities) (28:77):

> But seek the abode of the hereafter in that which Allah has given you, and do not neglect your portion of worldly life, and be kind even as Allah has been kind to you, and seek not corruption in the earth. Verily, Allah likes not the *mufsidun* [those who are mischief-makers, corrupted].

Islam is encouraging of work and productive effort to make legal profit. Indeed, the Quran is clear about the compatibility of prayer and profit (62:10): 'And when the prayer is finished, then may you disperse through the land, and seek of the bounty of Allah: and remember Allah frequently that you may prosper'. Rodinson (1966), a French Marxist, by appealing to the textual analysis of Islamic sources and the economic history of the Islamic world, demonstrated that Muslims had never had any problems with the idea of making money. According to Rodinson there are religions whose sacred texts discourage economic activity in general, but this is certainly not the case with the Quran. The Quran looks with favour upon commercial activity, confining itself to condemning fraudulent practices and requiring abstention from trade during certain religious festivals.

The Prophet, in another Hadith, once said that nine-tenths of all *rizk* (the bounty of God, which includes income) is derived from commerce. That, to a large extent, explains the drive of Muslims over the centuries to meet their economic needs through commerce, industry, agriculture and various forms of free enterprise. Profits are very much a part of such activities, provided they are lawfully obtained (*halal*). However, profits cannot overshadow the duties of brotherhood, solidarity, charity and they are, of course, subject to zakat (purifying alms).

The bottom line is that Islam is based on the paradigm of free choice, not coercion or autocracy. In Islam, freedom extends to work, property and the choice of how to use one's capabilities and resources.

The fundamental principle of free choice was boosted by the limitation of the Islamic state by the Quran. There was no government intervention in the economy except to expose fraud, punish theft or nullify *riba* (usury). Traditional Islam preserves free choice by limiting the scope of state intervention.

The institution of market supervision (*hisba*) is of particular interest. By including a long chapter on the functions of *al-Muhtasib*, the state officer in charge of the moral and economic supervision of the market, the Islamic scholar Al-Mawardi circumscribes the extent of state intervention in the economy. For him, the market supervisor is simply a coordinator of the marketplace to ensure that it operates on the principles of 'enjoining the right and forbidding the wrong'. This is a moral rather than an economic function. The functions of the supervisor in the economic realm are restricted to certain regulations, the inspection of weights and measures, the quality of products and the uprightness of contracts. Traditional Islam rejects any government intervention in the private economic sphere. For example, taxing the faithful is forbidden by the Quran and tariffs are not encouraged. The Prophet limits government intervention to fraud, which is something that falls naturally within the field of justice. This philosophy of economic freedom is very strong in Islam. For the Abbasids (the second of the two great dynasties of the Muslim Empire of the Caliphate, 750–1258), for example, customs duties were considered an impiety. For Al-Mawardi, state functions are limited to four: the army, border control, public administration and the treasury. Any direct intervention of the state in the economy is discouraged. For the historian Ibn Khaldun (1981), the state must confine itself to its natural functions: it should never compete with the private sector. He argues that the functions of the state are defence, law, public safety, money and politics.

In traditional Islam, free choice should not be hampered by heavy taxation. In the Quran there is no compulsory taxation. Ibn Khaldun (1996) anticipates the results of the Laffer curve, when he tells us that it is low taxation that brings the greatest revenue. In the same vein, for Ibn Abi Al-Rabi, a ninth-century Muslim scholar, economic flourishing requires that people keep their word and do not incur debts. So, for him, the state must always have a balanced budget. This view is correct, since government borrowing leads to the abuse of power by allowing the state to expand its remit and undermine the freedom of individuals. It also undermines civil society and breeds corruption.

State-directed monetary policy is a big impediment to free choice because government can control the economy through monetary policy, which is not possible if gold is used as money in an essentially private system. In contrast to conventional monetary policy, a traditional Islamic economic system based on gold does not suffer from the evils of seigniorage (the interest benefit to a bank from printing money).

Overall, Islamic traditions and teachings are not in conflict with a market-oriented economy inspired by free choice and profit motive.

The rule of law and contract

Free markets need protection of property rights and the rule of law to operate. Well-defined property rights, including procedures for recognition, alienation and inheritance, are basic elements for the establishment of a market economy. Private property is not simply recognised in Islam, it is sacred. The Quran mentions property 86 times, for example: 'And do not eat up your property among yourselves for vanities nor use it as bait for the judges with intent that ye may eat up wrongfully and knowingly a little of [other] people's property' (2:188). The Prophet in his farewell pilgrimage stated (see Haykal 1976: 486): 'O Men, your lives and your property shall be inviolate until you meet your Lord. The safety of your lives and of your property shall be as inviolate as this holy day and holy month.'

In contrast to socialism, Islam enshrines private property as a sacred trust. According to the Quran, everything in this world belongs to Allah. Individuals, to whom Allah has entrusted the world, have their own property and Muslims have to respect the private property of others as well. 'O you who believe! Enter not houses other than your own, until ye have asked permission and saluted those in them' (24:27).

Therefore, that concept of private property, well-established among the Semitic peoples, is taken as a given by the Quran. Rather than modifying the concept of property, the Quran specifies the terms for its wholesome and just enjoyment and employment.

Property should not be used wastefully nor in a way that will deprive others of their justly acquired property (2:188). When one holds the property of others in trust, for example for orphans, one should not divert it to one's own personal benefit (2:2; 4:10); and one should not turn over one's own property to those incapable of managing it (2:5). When orphans mature they should be given control of their own property (2:6). Inheritance rights are not only respected (4:33), but expanded to include women (4:7). Property rights of women are as sacred as those of men in other cases as well (4:24; 4:32) and the treatment of women as chattels is prohibited (4:19).

The Prophet emphasised the importance of property rights in his farewell pilgrimage by declaring to the assembled masses: 'Nothing shall be legitimate to a Muslim which belongs to a fellow Muslim unless it was given freely and willingly.' The Quran guaranteed the rights of women to property and to freedom to contract, and even a share in inheritances, fourteen centuries before some states in America granted married women the right to property at all.

Free markets need the rule of law to operate because they do not operate by commands, but by individual choices made under laws. In modern times we understand the rule of law to apply to all equally, even to the monarch and to parliament. Abu Bakr, upon his inauguration as Caliph (successor to the Prophet Muhammad) said (Ahmad 1996):

> It is true that I have been elected your amir [ruler] ... If I give you a command in accord with the Quran and the practice of the Prophet, obey me. But if I give you a command departing from the Quran or the practice of the Prophet, you owe me no obedience, but must correct me. Truth is righteousness, and falsehood is treason.

Abu Bakr's comment is extremely important. In this comment he identifies the essence of the difference between ancient systems of command and the decision-making process under the rule of law. In a law-based economy, a single set of laws or rules governs decision-making and people operate not on the basis of commands tailored to specific transactions, but on their free choice within the scope afforded by universally applied laws: this is precisely the Islamic system.

Islamic law in general is a framework in which individuals and intermediate institutions of society make contracts to govern their relationships and actions, including their business enterprises. Thus the fulfilling of contracts appears immediately after prayer and charity in the list of what defines righteousness (2:177). The formal and informal institutions that arose through this framework of Islamic law, which is so favourable to enterprise and free markets, account for the success of Muslim Spain.

Contracts of various types are regulated by the Sharia and are subject to the concepts of *halal* and *haram*. Contracts are essentially predicated on the free will of the parties and must manifest the true expression of their intent. Economic activities based on implied contracts are also balanced by a variety of what would now be called equitable principles to insure against undue influence and lack of fairness, which relate to questions of competence, validity, rescission and damages.

Thus, it could be said that in Islam every contract is basically lawful as long it does not oppose any explicit text of the Quran and Sunna. Allah says in the Holy Quran at Surat al-Maidah: 'O you who believe fulfil your obligations' (5:1). A Muslim who breaches contractual obligations does not only breach a contract but also an express command of Allah. Therefore, it would expose him not only to civil liability but also to divine retribution.

Competition

The Quran encouraged competition in benefiting from God's bounties. This concerns not only the life hereafter but also the worldly life.

Islam encourages competition by limiting distortions to prices and state control of prices. The Prophet was equally sensitive to the rights of the sellers and he was against price fixing at times of scarcity.

State interference in the market was limited. *Al Muhtasib,* the highest economic representative of the governing body in a city, had an extremely limited range of action in the economy. As far as Caliph Omar I was concerned, the state must be limited to defence, justice, the control of weights and measures and public works; and it should never compete with the private sector, which should be left in full liberty. This resonates with Adam Smith. For Omar ibn Al Khattab, state intervention in trade was an abuse. The state does not function as a business, but should govern – a very different function.

The Prophet was greatly concerned with the material conditions of the market so as to make commerce as free and equal as possible. He was involved in the inspection of the marketplace to check the accuracy of weights and measures, and he assigned particular places for different mongers in the market. The objective of the Prophet's policy was to guarantee fair economic dealings. As an illustration, we can refer to the Prophet's advice to his companions on the issue of meeting merchants from neighbouring villages and towns. A city merchant would often meet the merchants that were visiting from villages on the outskirts of the city and buy their merchandise at unfairly low prices. The Prophet interdicted such trades in his statements: 'Do not go out to meet riders [merchants from villages] and a city dweller should not sell things to a desert dweller'. This kind of sale was illegal if there was no choice given to the seller to cancel the transaction if he found that he has been wronged or treated unfairly after discovering the real market price of his merchandise.

Islam also rejected any kind of monopoly or *ihtikar.* The Prophet Muhammad made explicit and specific statements about prohibiting monopoly. For example, he said: 'Whoever withholds food (in order to raise its price), has certainly erred!' (reported in Hadith Sahih Muslim). He also said: 'Whoever strives to increase the cost [of products] for Muslims, Allah, the Exalted, will seat him in the centre of the Fire on the Day of Resurrection' (Hadith Ahmad in Musnad 5:27 and Al-Hakim in Al-Mustadrak 13-2:12). In another Hadith the Messenger of Allah says: 'What an evil person is the one who withholds! If Allah causes the prices to drop, he would be saddened, and if He causes them to climb, He would be excited' (Hadith al-Bayhaqi in al-Sunan al-Kubra).

Explaining the deviation from the pro-market tradition of Islam

Deviations from the principles of a free-market economy can come from a number of directions: the misinterpretation of Islam's original tenets; the collusion between politicians and clergy; socialism and the excesses of state intervention; and the misapplication of liberal policies.

Misinterpretation of Islamic tenets

Over the hundreds of years of the classical Islamic era, departures from early Muslim teachings accumulated until the 'closing of the door to ijtihad' (the exercise of personal interpretation and judgement based on the Quran and the Sunna). This precipitated the loss of dynamism in Islamic jurisprudence, the stagnation of the law and the fall of Islam relative to the West (it was about the time that ijtihad was being abandoned by Muslims that the West began adopting concepts such as the rule of law, eventually leading to its Renaissance).

Islamic socialists have long pointed to the importance of social justice, and many have drawn an inference in favour of state-granted minimum incomes, and even a large role for high government expenditures. Others have cited Quranic prohibitions on usury (interest) as an indication of anti-capitalist sentiment in Islam – even as an insurmountable problem for contemporary Islamic liberalism.

It is true that the Quran has a strong emphasis on social justice and this has led some modern Muslim intellectuals to sympathise with socialism and its promise of a classless society. But a careful reading of the Quran would not support such 'Islamo-socialism'. For example, it warned that it was not wise to 'covet those things in which God hath bestowed his gifts more freely on some of you than on others: to men is allotted what they earn and to women what they earn; but ask God of His bounty, for God hath full knowledge of all things' (4:32).

Muslim scripture takes it as given that there will be rich and poor people in society and, in a sense, assures us that such disparity will and should remain by actively supporting the rights to private property and inheritance.

The zakat was interpreted as an egalitarian tax to collectivise wealth, discouraging work and productivity. However, technically, it is not a tax. Rather, it is a charitable contribution, which the faith requires, set at 2.5 per cent of accumulated wealth beyond a subsistence level of wealth after allowing for the tools of a person's trade and current inventories. It is not an assessment against income. As such, it does not discourage productivity but discourages idle wealth. Furthermore, the levels of the assessment are not confiscatory. So, while it provides a safety net for the poor, it in no way equalises wealth nor unduly penalises the rich. The term *zakat* itself comes from a word that means 'to purify'. The return of a small portion of one's wealth to the general community therefore purifies the rest of one's wealth from any taint that an initial inequality of assets might suggest. The needs of the unfortunate are met without impairing the productivity of those God has blessed materially. Finally, zakat is an act of charity (though one required by the faith) and not a collectivisation of wealth by a central authority. It is primarily a voluntary act of piety and a far cry from the levels of tax that most modern-day taxpayers experience.

Contrary to other religions, Islam rejects monastic asceticism that glorifies poverty and suffering: neither poverty nor wealth are a proof of virtue. Both are trials of one's commitment to the higher spiritual order. The rejection of asceticism is not an invitation to hedonistic consumption, however.

Besides misinterpretation, another reason for the deviation of Islam from the free-market economic tradition is the rejection of innovation, be it political, intellectual or technical. Muhammad, a trader himself, sprinkled the Quran with reflections on the market. Kuran (2010) makes the intriguing case that the evolution of Islamic law was at the root of the problem. Its strictures, he claims, inhibited the emergence of the institutions of modern capitalism as they developed in Europe; and the Middle East is suffering for that failure to this day.

How did that happen? When it first developed, Islamic law was actually quite progressive and orientated towards the market economy. It allowed for the easy formation of partnerships and clear rules to guide commercial behaviour in a fair way. However, over the centuries, Islamic law fell out of touch with the times and failed to adapt to the new world commercial order that developed from Europe. While Europeans were creating innovative institutions that allowed them to amass and mobilise resources on a mammoth scale – such as joint stock companies and modern banking systems – Islamic law in the Middle East prevented these same institutions from forming. Partnership practices, which allow any partner to dissolve the arrangement, and inheritance laws, which mandate that the assets of the deceased transfer to particular family members, discouraged the emergence of the modern corporation, for example, by restricting the ability of Muslims to form long-standing business organisations. Ordering death for apostasy made it extremely difficult to do business in non-Muslim legal systems.

Even after strict Islamic law was eventually liberalised in many parts of the Muslim world, its structures had already done their damage, leaving the Middle East devoid of the strong private sectors it needed. When Arab countries then tried to copy Western economic institutions, such as courts with European commercial codes, they proved a poor fit. Having not emerged naturally from society, the imported institutions did not work as they did back home. In modern times, that left the state to play an overly powerful role in the Middle East's economic development. This did not produce the same amazing results as the Asian model based on trade and entrepreneurship.

Colonisation and socialism

The Ottoman Empire and the European colonisers generally sought to modernise existing economic relations. The Ottoman Empire during the *Tanzimat* era (an era of reorganisation of the Ottoman Empire from 1839 to 1876) showed that it is possible to reform Islamic law, but that it could trigger significant opposition. European colonisation also tried to change practices regulated by Islamic law and promote living by Western law, but this faced rejection by indigenous populations.

The legal tradition of the colonisers played a role as an incubator. Muslim countries inherited their broad legal traditions from their colonisers (British common law, French civil law, German code, socialist law, and indigenous Nordic or Scandinavian legal traditions). It is generally accepted that British colonisation bequeathed a more liberal judicial tradition than the French, Spanish and Russian (Soviet) traditions. So Muslim countries (for example, Bahrain, Oman, Qatar, Kuwait, UAE, Malaysia and Saudi Arabia) that were colonised by Britain had relatively decentralised systems and limited government; others (for example, Guinea, Senegal, Mali, Algeria, Djibouti, Mauritania, Niger, Syria,

Chad, Lebanon, Tunisia and Morocco) that were colonised by France inherited centralised government opposed to a free-market economy. Colonisation has created a form of path dependency. Muslim countries colonised by the French, Spanish and Russians/Soviets have generally followed socialist and centralised models (for example, Algeria and Syria). The adoption of the socialist and centralised model was justified by the fallacy that the command economy can better provide for the material needs of a society. It was also encouraged by the Cold War and the opposition between capitalism and Soviet socialism.

Economies based on rent-seeking have taken hold. This eliminates competition and promotes what is often described as 'crony capitalism'. These systems block the productive activity of entrepreneurs and promote unproductive activities, as well as predation. Independence has allowed the emergence of economies managed and controlled by small groups of families (Saud in Saudi Arabia, Sheikh Sa'ad in Kuwait), political parties such as the Ba'ath in Iraq, groups of soldiers and coup plotters (for example, in Egypt and Syria) or an ethnic minority (for example, Jordan). This model of a predatory state has often been facilitated by the redistribution of some of the oil wealth to buy the legitimacy of the regime. This has involved the creation of large numbers of civil service posts with higher salaries being paid than in the private sector.

The dominant model of Muslim and Arab countries reproduced the models of the Arabic and Ottoman empires. This model rehabilitates an aristocracy of the state with a large public sector, high levels of redistribution and a system characterised by cronyism and corruption. Independence often led to dirigisme, socialism and hyper-nationalism. This arose largely as a result of causes external to Islam. Indeed, it is in the nature of governments and military dictatorships in general whether or not they are coupled to religious authorities.

The failure of market economies to become consolidated in Muslim countries is the result of a sort of forced Westernisation, which resulted in the development of socialist and rent-seeking economies hostile to the principles of free markets.

Fake liberalisation

When liberalisation happens, it tends to be very slowly. First there appears what might be described as 'superficial liberalism': the import of consumer goods of good quality is liberalised somewhat. This is progress, but it is not liberalism. Another step, often under pressure from the IMF, is privatisation. The actual implementation takes years because the process clashes with vested interests. There are many monopolies that are resistant, reinforced by the protected jobs they represent. All this has nothing to do with the Quran. The disappointing outcome of failed policies of privatisation is mainly due to certain institutional prerequisites not being observed: the rule of law, the abolition of price controls and the presence of free competition.

Indeed, privatisation was carried out mostly in the context of regulatory and legal uncertainty. The absence or weakness of law enforcement due to corruption and bureaucracy made it difficult to eliminate monopolistic practices, ensure investor protection, allow for the creation and liquidation of companies, and promote vibrant trade. Moreover, the lack of competence, transparency and independence of the judiciary did not incentivise investment because the property rights of investors were not secure. In Algeria, for example, justice systems are often used by businesses to drive competitors out of business and maintain market dominance. In short, privatisation transactions take place in a context where the legal environment is unsuitable or unable to protect private property and freedom of contract, hence their poor record.

The lack of freedom in pricing has also created uncertainty. It was therefore unrealistic to expect the development of a vibrant private sector. The privatisation of major utilities (for example, water and electricity) in Muslim countries was often put in place while prices were controlled. This explains the lack of investor interest, especially given the extent of investment required. Moreover, trade liberalisation after privatisation creates more uncertainty for the purchasers of former public enterprises. As such, the liberalisation of prices and trade should normally be undertaken before the implementation of privatisation programmes.

Privatisations have often been undertaken without the establishment of mechanisms to enable effective competition. Consequently, they led to the transformation of a public monopoly into private monopoly, which was both inefficient and not accepted by the public. In the absence of free competition, when prices were liberalised they tended to increase dramatically and this caused social unrest. From this perspective, the success of privatisation depends on creating an environment conducive to healthy and open competition. It is therefore necessary to prevent the creation of cartels, monopolies and other restrictive business practices.

Thus, the failure of privatisation and partial liberalisation in the Muslim world has created resentment of a free-market economy among Muslim citizens.[1] The transfer of ownership from a public monopoly that is bureaucratic and corrupt to a private monopoly which does not benefit Muslim citizens explains the present resistance to free-market reforms. Worse, the serious social crises that have resulted in job losses and rising prices for some goods and services have not only strengthened the hostility and mistrust of people, but have also sometimes resulted in a reversal of the process of privatisation with companies being renationalised. This weakens the market economy and once again strengthens state intervention.

---

1   Editor's note: it should be noted that this is in no way unique to the Muslim world. A very similar phenomenon can be seen, for example, in South and Central America.

Conclusion

There have been many theories of how the Middle East lost out economically to the West. Many people have claimed that Islam itself is biased against a free-market economy as a way of producing development and prosperity. This argument falls flat. If Islam was inherently anti-commerce, how can we explain the vibrancy of the economies of the Muslim world in the centuries after the Arab conquests? And, in modern times, certain Islamic nations, especially Malaysia and Indonesia, have been among the world's fastest growing economies. Remember, Muhammad himself was a merchant before he became the Prophet, and Mecca, the first city of Islam, had been a major centre of the caravan trade.

As we have shown, the problem is not the incompatibility between the tenets of Islam and the principles of a free economy, but the deviation from the liberal tradition of early Islam. The rest of the Arab world will have to follow the example of Dubai as well as Turkey, Malaysia and Indonesia. The incoming leadership of the Arab world has been left with the unenviable task of first building the foundation necessary for vibrant, modern and competitive economies. Such revived economies should then rediscover the tradition of free trade throughout the whole Muslim world and beyond. A global free trade area implies deep institutional reform that is conducive to economic liberty and a free-market economy in order to create the employment and economic growth that is so much needed in the region.

References

Ahmad, I. A. (1996) Islam, market economy, and the rule of law. Second International Symposium on Liberalism in Ankara, 18–19 May.

Haykal, M. H. (1976) *The Life of Muhammad*. University of Chicago Press.

Khaldun, I. (1981) *The Muqaddimah* (translated by F. Rosental), 5th edn. Princeton University Press.

Kuran, T. (2010) *The Long Divergence: How Islamic Law Held Back the Middle East*. Princeton University Press.

Rodinson, M. (1966) *Islam et Capitalism*. Paris: Editions du Seuil.

10 ISLAMIC FINANCE: BETWEEN THE REALITY AND THE IDEAL

Youcef Maouchi

Introduction

More than 40 years after its emergence, Islamic finance continues to draw attention. Advocates of what is seen as a different, ethical and solidarity-based alternative finance continue to make enthusiastic assessments of an industry that has been rightly described as having its roots and spirit in Islam, a religion that is over 1400 years old.

With $1,658 billion in global assets in 2014 and near double-digit annual growth, Islamic finance provokes interest, not only in Muslim countries but also in the West. In an era in which Western states are in need of fresh capital and with conventional finance going through a crisis, a new form of finance claiming to ally business and ethics is more than welcome. The most striking evidence of this interest is the move made by David Cameron in 2013 pledging to make London one of the world's 'great capitals of Islamic finance' when he unveiled Treasury plans to create a £200 million Islamic bond.

Commonly referred to as 'interest-free' banking and finance, Islamic finance is supposed to be more than just a ban on interest. Its advocates see it as the miracle solution for today's problems. Some Islamic finance figures argue that there is no need to brand it as 'Islamic' because it is first and foremost an ethical, socially responsible form of finance. It is a form of finance that emphasises a participatory approach aimed at businesspeople and entrepreneurs and which invests in the real economy. Besides these enthusiastic views, Islamic finance faces severe criticisms. The reproaches are directed towards the current practices of Islamic banks and financial institutions. In theory they are supposed to follow a different model of financial intermediation, based on partnership, but, in practice, this is not the case: they rely mostly on debt instruments. There is an ongoing debate about the form and substance of Islamic finance. In form, Islamic finance seems to be different from conventional finance, but in substance there are many similarities. Mahmoud El-Gamal, one of the most well-recognised critics of the actual practices of Islamic finance, writes that by 'attempting to replicate the substance of contemporary financial practice using premodern contract forms, Islamic finance has arguably failed to serve the objectives of Islamic Law [of aiming to achieve justice and equity in economics]' (El-Gamal 2006: xii). He argues that the 'Islamic' in 'Islamic finance' should relate to the social and economic ends of financial transactions, rather than the contractual mechanics through which financial ends are achieved.

While acknowledging the critics, defenders of Islamic finance justify current practices by referring to the 'unfair competition' with long-established conventional banks and the not-well-suited legal and fiscal frameworks. The solution stressed is the need to 'Islamise' the economies in which Islamic finance institutions operate in order that they can fully achieve the original aspirations. However, while there is some truth in their diagnosis, the solution proposed is far from harmless.

Islamic finance: an overview

Every religion has a certain number of principles, including in the economic and social sphere. Just as Christianity has social teaching, which in the Catholic Church is more formally laid down as 'Catholic social teaching', Islam includes its own vision of economics and society. Islamic finance is said to be the practical expression of the economy seen through an Islamic lens. It is crystallised in the maxims *al-kharaj bi al-dhaman* and *al-ghanum bi al-gharam* ('one has to bear loss, if any, if he wants to get any profit over his investment' (Ayub 2007: 81)).

This vision centres on *riba* (interest), *gharar* (uncertainty) and *maysir* (gambling). Transactions are forbidden if one party is compensated with interest or if the existence of the object of the transaction is not certain or under contractual terms that are unclear. Such rules exist to prevent unjust enrichment. Along with these limitations, Islam forbids consuming, producing or financing *haram* (unlawful) goods and services such as alcohol, pork, pornography and gambling.

Despite these restrictions, Islamic finance responds to the same needs as conventional finance does, linking demand for and supply of investable funds. Like conventional finance, Islamic finance, which is described as the application of Islamic law in modern times, relies on basic financial mechanisms (contracts) which, however, have to be compatible with the teachings of Islam. These mechanisms are *mudharaba, musharaka, bay' salam, murabaha* and *ijara*. The *mudharaba* contract is very close to the conventional venture capital financing whereby the investor shares in the risk of the venture and participates very directly in its initiation. *Musharaka* financing is very similar to conventional private equity financing. *Bay' salam* is similar to a conventional forward contract. *Murabaha* is a cost plus sale and the *ijara* is similar to a leasing operation.

It is on these five basic simple contracts and their various combinations that the majority of Islamic finance tools stand. These different contracts at the base of a range of complex financial tools can be classified into two groups: debt-like and equity contracts.

Mudharaba and *musharaka* are considered as profit-and-loss sharing instruments and are non-debt-creating in the sense that the finance user is not obliged to pay back the total amount of financing. *Bay' salam, murabaha* and *ijara* are viewed as debt-like financing because the financed party has a debt to the financier to whom it must pay back the entire amount of the received financing. The amount of financing and reimbursement is defined at the beginning; it is a debt from the viewpoint of the party receiving the finance.

As noted by Dar and Presley (2000), profit-and-loss sharing schemes dominate the Islamic finance literature. These schemes, as their name indicates, are contractual arrangements between two or more parties enabling them to mobilise funds for project financing and share the resulting profits and losses. They represent the true interpretation of Islamic finance. If the ban on interest is the direct implication of the Islamic vision of the economy, which seems to be a moral justification for the establishment of a banking and financial system different from the conventional one, advocates of Islamic finance have made the profit-and-loss sharing scheme its practical expression.

Thus, the difference between Islamic finance and conventional finance is not just a matter of banned interest or forbidden investments in *haram* industries. Advocates of Islamic finance aimed to build a form of finance different and distinguishable from conventional finance by its entrepreneurial approach and the use of investment and partnership tools, i.e. a form of participatory finance.

Emphasis on the participatory dimension of Islamic finance resulted in profit-and-loss share contracts receiving the bulk of attention from Islamic scholars. These contracts have been branded as the most Islamic of the Islamic finance tools.

If it is true that profit-and-loss share, especially *mudharaba* and *musharaka,* were used in early Islam and that all the contracts used in Islamic finance can, more or less, be traced back to the early times of Islam, the experience of Islamic banking is a recent one. The first successful Islamic bank, Mith Ghamr, was established in 1963 in Egypt. So, why does the profit-and-loss share contract receive so much attention and why is it considered more in line with Islam. Before looking at this particular question, a detour into the origin of Islamic finance and Islamic law is necessary.

The origins of Islamic finance: the Sharia

Despite the fact that the Quran and the Sunna are considered as the basis on which *Sharia* (Islamic law) is built, the Quran does not contain any doctrine or system of law. Although there are some specific injunctions regarding marriage and inheritance, most of the time the will of God is expressed in the form of general principles. The Quran provides a set of normative principles while the Sunna is a sort of case law decided by the Prophet in light of the Quran.

In the early centuries of Islam, there was still no system of Islamic law, let alone an Islamic law governing contracts. Chéhata noted that 'during the first centuries of Islam, there was not even a germ of Islamic law. It seems that Muslim communities lived under customary law that prevailed in the regions where they lived'.

Islamic law (as a body of law and science) does not appear in history until the advent of the Abbasids in 750 AD, which saw Islamic civilisation reaching its apogee (from around 775 to 861 AD). Hence the question: from where did this law come? What happened over the first two centuries of Islam?

According to Hourani (1993: 99), at the times of the caliphs, there were two distinct processes by which laws were produced. Firstly, monarchs, their governors and special delegates, the *Qadis* (judges), reached decisions and resolved disputes on the basis of laws and local customs of the region in which they were living and working. Simultaneously, converted and committed Muslims tried to subject all human actions to the judgements and the light of their religion to develop a system of ideal human behaviour. When society faced a new problem to which a solution could not be found in the Quran and the Sunna, Muslim jurists and scholars issued legal opinions (*fatwas*) based on their understanding and interpretation of the basic codes. But, at that time there was still no agreement on what sources should be used to discover law. The decisive step in defining the relationship between the different bases for legal decisions was taken by the great Muslim jurist Al-Shafi'i. According to Hourani (1993: 101):

> Confronted with a new situation, those who were qualified to exercise their reason (opinion-jurists) should proceed by analogy (*qiyas*): They should try to find some element in the situation which was similar, in a relevant way, to an element in a situation on which a ruling already existed. Such a disciplined exercise of reason was known as *ijtihad*. When there was general agreement as a result of such an exercise of reason, then this consensus (*ijma*) would be regarded as having the status of certain and unquestionable truth.

Regarding contracts, Islamic jurists (*fuqaha)* categorised them into classes with their own distinctive rules. It is generally argued that Islamic law knows no general theory of contract. Hence, Chéhata (1971: 44) describes Islamic law as an empirical law: 'In its external structure', he writes, 'Islamic law is a sort of a case law.' This argument is based on the fact that the *fiqh* (Islamic jurisprudence) books do not contain any general contract theory. Therefore, the development of Islamic contract law is the result of the method undertaken by Muslim jurists to develop a system categorising the contracts. They tried to make every contract stand on a moral basis compliant with the Islamic vision.

Broadly, these contracts were scrutinised from two perspectives. They were scrutinised for their legal validity (ranging from *sahih* 'valid' to *batil* 'null and void'). And they were scrutinised from a religious perspective (ranging from *wajib* 'obligatory' to *haram* 'forbidden' or 'unlawful').

The ideal of Islamic finance

The literature on the implementation of Islamic finance has sought to justify, economically and socially, the necessity of adopting economic practices that are compatible with the teachings of Islam and exclusively based on a profit-and-loss sharing paradigm, using profit-and-loss sharing contracts.

This is how the first wave of Islamic finance literature has tackled the issue of proving the superiority of an Islamic financial system *vis-à-vis* its Western counterpart relying on interest lending. According to this literature, a system based on a profit-and-loss sharing paradigm will foster investment in the real economy and lead to a more stable system, resilient to shocks while being fairer and more efficient.

This literature appeared in the 1980s and tried to prove that, if interest payment were replaced by a profit-and-loss sharing scheme, the level of investment in the economy would be enhanced. The rationale behind this idea could be linked to the venture capital industry in the West that has helped the establishment of huge corporations, for example in the information technology sector. In fact, as stated by Kuran (1993: 309), the main idea was that a banking system that bases its financing decisions on the long-term prospects and profitability of a venture may accept projects that do not get finance in the conventional system which bases decisions on creditworthiness.

The corollary of this idea is that there is no justification for a capital provider to claim a positive return if the business that is being financed fails. This argument was pushed further by showing that, in poor economic conditions, the profit-and-loss sharing approach will be more resilient as the returns paid to the financiers depend directly on the returns of the underlying projects being financed. The shocks that will hit the asset side of a financial institution (a fall in the value of assets due to losses being made by businesses) will be absorbed by losses on the liabilities side (those who have money invested in the institution will bear losses too). The fortunes of the depositors become linked with those of the borrowers so that the financial institution is more robust.

Thus, a profit-and-loss sharing system is seen as fairer as the borrower will no longer bear the risk alone but will share it with the financier.

But by far the most powerful argument in favour of Islamic finance has been the idea of linking the financial sector to the real sector. Unlike conventional finance, all Islamic financial instruments are linked to existing or potential real assets. Thus Islamic finance directly finances the real economy rather than becoming involved with speculating in and dealing with financial assets derived from debt-based financial assets. With Islamic finance we would get back to the original purpose of finance.

Yousef and Aggarwal (2000: 100) noted that the advocates of Islamic finance expected Islamic financial institutions to perform the function of allocating investment funds to long-term productive projects and to favour small entrepreneurs who do not have access to credit. In sum, Islamic banks were viewed as an engine or a tool to move Muslim countries out of poverty.

The reality takes over from the ideal

Notwithstanding the fact that it aimed to be different and distinguishable from conventional finance by its entrepreneurial approach and use of investment and partnership tools, Islamic finance, claiming to be a form of participatory finance, seems to have only succeeded in giving different names for practices from which it wanted to depart. For El-Gamal (2006: 24), Islamic finance, is just an 'inefficient replication of conventional finance, always one step behind [conventional] developments.'

A quick look at the practice of Islamic financial institutions shows a real gap between the aspiration to establish a profit-and-loss sharing system and the practice, relying mostly on debt-like instruments (also known as mark-up-based instruments). Although the debt-like instruments are not contrary to the teachings of Islam, the fact that instruments other than profit-and-loss sharing contracts, and especially *murabaha* contracts, dominate Islamic banks' assets suggests a failure for the advocates of the 'sharing' paradigm. An analysis of the Islamic Development Bank's asset portfolio for 1976 to 2004 showed that 91 per cent of its financial transactions were not in profit-and-loss sharing contracts. *Murabaha*'s share in Islamic banks' asset portfolios in Indonesia between 2006 and 2007 was 55 per cent. Their share was 48 per cent in Malaysia and 44 per cent in Pakistan. In some Middle Eastern and North African (MENA) countries *murabaha* constitutes more than 90 per cent of financing schemes. In others it is just below 50 per cent. Across the entire MENA region, the share of *murabaha* in total financing is 75 per cent. The trend is not reversing.

This situation has led some critics to reproach Islamic financiers for not practising what they preach.

Even that part of Islamic finance that has enjoyed undisputed success – the well-known *sukuk* referred to as 'Islamic bonds' are not immune to controversy in relation to the risk-sharing versus risk-transfer question.

With regard to this form of contract, the 'form' versus 'substance' debate is trickier and technical. The core question is whether the *sukuk* are asset-based or asset-backed structures.

Sukuk (plural of *sakk*) are 'certificates of equal value representing undivided shares in the ownership of tangible assets, usufructs and services or (in the ownership of) the assets of particular projects or special investment activity' (AAOIFI 2010: 238). Income to *sukuk*-holders is generated by trading or investing the 'underlying assets'. The ownership of the assets financed using a *sukuk* operation is supposed to be the core difference from conventional bond instruments which are pure debt securities. Thus bondholders own a debt and receive interest; *sukuk*-holders co-own an asset and earn profit.

Sukuk are financial tools generated by a combination of the basic contracts listed above. They can be structured following debt-based or equity-based principles and must undergo a screening process by Sharia scholars to ensure that they are Sharia compliant (that is free from elements that are prohibited, such as riba and *gharar* and from non-permissible activities).

In a recent study of 131 *sukuk* issues by 43 companies between 2006 to 2013 covering eight countries, Godlewski et al. (2014) found that debt-based *sukuk* accounted for 57 per cent of the sample. The major *sukuk* types in their sample were *ijara* (44 per cent) and *musharaka* (37 per cent), followed by *murabaha* (13 per cent).

While *sukuk* were considered the Islamic finance success story, growing from less than $8 billion in 2003 to $50 billion by mid 2007, the Islamic finance industry was shaken in 2008 by a paper published by Sheikh Taqi Usmani (2008), one of the leading Sharia scholars in Islamic finance. He stated that the majority of the *sukuk* in the market were not in line with the principles of Sharia.

After this statement, along with the default of some *sukuk* in the aftermath of the financial crisis, Islamic finance jargon developed to create a new categorisation of *sukuk*: asset-based and asset-backed *sukuk*.

The main difference involves the concept of a 'true sale'. In asset-backed *sukuk*, the originator (the issuer of the *sukuk*) sells the assets to a special purpose vehicle (SPV) that issues the *sukuk*. The SPV acts as a trustee for the *sukuk*-holder who does not have recourse to the originator. The *sukuk*-holder is a legal owner of the asset and receives revenues based on the performance of the underlying assets. In the asset-based *sukuk* there is no sale. The *sukuk*-holders have beneficial ownership of the assets. In the case of a shortfall in payments, the originator is liable. The *sukuk* structure incorporates an income and capital guarantee from the originator. Thus, the risk is not shared but falls on the financed party.

From this general picture of the practice of Islamic finance, it is clear that the use of debt-like instruments is the norm within the Islamic finance industry and there is a real gap between the theory of Islamic finance and its practice.

Bringing Islamic finance back on track

The lack of profit-and-loss sharing arrangements in the balance sheet of Islamic financial institutions prompted a second wave of literature that tried to understand and find solutions to the gap between the ideal form of Islamic finance and its practice.

This literature identifies several explanations for this gap. Some of these problems are summarised by Dar and Presley (2000: 3–4):

- Profit-and-loss sharing contracts are inherently vulnerable to agency problems as entrepreneurs have fewer incentives to make their businesses a success and to report the right amount of profit as compared with a self-financing owner-manager.
- Profit-and-loss sharing contracts require well-defined property rights to function efficiently – as the ownership interests in the venture from which the profits are being shared need to be clear and enforceable. Because in most Muslim countries property rights are not properly defined or protected, such contracts are deemed to be less attractive or fail if used.

- Islamic banks and investment companies have to offer relatively less risky modes of financing in the wake of severe competition from conventional banks and other financial institutions, which are already established and hence more competitive.
- This form of equity financing is difficult for short-term funding because of liquidity problems. This makes Islamic banks and other financial institutions rely on some other debt-like forms of financing.
- Unfair treatment in taxation is also considered to be a major obstacle in the use of profit-and-loss sharing arrangements. In most tax systems, profits are taxed while interest is exempt from tax at the level of the corporation on the grounds that it constitutes a cost item (though it may be taxed in the hands of the recipient).

While some of these problems are being addressed by scholars and bankers, they are not the ones emphasised by leading critics.

Some supporters of Islamic finance argue for a total Islamisation and standardisation of the economy to fit Islamic finance principles. For them, Islamic finance will only achieve its objectives through the imposition of a single financial system in line with Islamic ethics. In order for Islamic banks and financial institutions to fully operate on a partnership scheme, the context in which they evolve must be completely riba-free (that is, without payment of interest in any form) and must leave no room for conventional banks. If today's Islamic banks move towards profit-and-loss sharing instruments, it is only an intermediate step before the full Islamisation of the economy.

For instance, while addressing the extensive use of the *murabaha*, justice Taqi Usmani (2002: 41) writes:

It should never be overlooked that, originally, *murabahah* is not a mode of financing. It is only a device to escape from 'interest' and not an ideal instrument for carrying out the real economic objectives of Islam. Therefore, this instrument should be used as a transitory step taken in the process of the Islamisation of the economy, and its use should be restricted only to those cases where *mudarabah* or *musharakah* are not practicable.

Though the idea of full Islamisation of the economy could be linked to the failure of Islamic banks to deliver their original objectives, this view has its roots in a more radical vision, which led to the creation of an Islamic finance industry in the first place. It is believed that most, though not all, of the problems of the Islamic world (and to a large extent capitalism) are rooted in the practice of lending with interest. Among these problems are unemployment, inflation, poverty amid plenty, increasing inequality and recurrent business cycles. It is thought that these problems could be solved by abolishing interest and replacing it with profit sharing. We end up in a vicious circle: lending with interest is the root of the problems, thus we should create an alternative system. Because this alternative system does not really solve the original problems, we should go further and make it the only one.

However, we should be highly sceptical of attempts to create a fully Islamic financial system. Its effects could worsen the problems the Islamic world and finance are facing.

Firstly, the example of countries that attempted the full Islamisation of their economy does not seem to be a total success. As noted by Khan (2010: 813): 'Islamic Banks in Pakistan, Sudan and Iran, whose governments favour Islamic Banking over conventional, all rely on non-PLS [profit-and-loss sharing] financing forms.'

This is for a number of reasons. The most important is the very nature of Islamic law, which as described earlier bears a close resemblance to common law. On this topic El-Gamel (2006: 16) brought to attention an interesting quote from Rosen: 'in Pakistan and Sudan the simple use of Islamic law as an arm of the state has slipped through the fingers of those at the center. The reason, I believe, is that these regimes have been trying to apply a common law variant as if it were a civil law system.'

So, the question remains: how would a total Islamisation of an economy change the way Islamic finance works today? This important question brings us to the significant effects such a move could have.

Imposing a finance model without interest at a country level means that individuals and companies would have a restricted choice in terms of the contracts that they can use. They must rely on the basic Islamic-approved Sharia-compliant contracts. Thus, they are forced to operate in a predefined way by the state. It would question the very nature of freedom of contract.

It should be remembered that the goal of any contract is to achieve mutual gain. In finance, contracts allow us to make economic transactions that make very-long-term projects possible, even if the future remains fundamentally unknown.

The contract itself has a form of insurance role. If something goes wrong during the contract, there is recourse to the other party and this helps to reduce the uncertainty inherent to economic life. Any attempt to force individuals to achieve their goals in predefined ways may have adverse effects on transactions and trade. This will surely slow down economic activity and would have the opposite effect to that for which advocates of Islamic finance hope.

Conclusion

The promoters of Islamic finance envisaged a system that was compliant with what is believed to be a fair and ethical view of economic activity. Despite the huge potential of Islamic finance and its double-digit growth rates in the recent past, the appraisal of the phenomenon is mixed. The theorists continue to call for more profit-and-loss sharing finance, while the practitioners are failing to implement the original project.

Different reasons are identified as the main barrier to a fully Islamic finance. These dangers, far from being exclusive to Islamic finance, are encountered in different ways in conventional finance.

Trying to apply today a set of contracts developed and used ten centuries ago in a very different context is not an easy task. Yet, it seems that the advocates of the profit-and-loss sharing paradigm suffer from a nirvana fallacy as they compare the world as it exists to an imaginary perfect world. Their ideal world is a world without conventional banks and without lending with interest, but the real world is a world where Islamic banks are competing with conventional banks and people have access to different forms of finance.

Due to the fact that, in the real world, Islamic financial institutions are not fond of profit-and-loss sharing and conventional banks lending with interest do exist, such banks will always be identified as a principal and irremediable cause of the underuse of profit-and-loss sharing.

But, the conclusions drawn from this approach could be dangerous. Forbidding the real world will not bring about the ideal world and, meanwhile, it would prevent Islamic financial institutions from operating.

Most importantly, this literature failed to pay attention to the security of capital and the protection of the financiers. Despite the fact that some authors have highlighted it, the institutional environment in which the majority of Islamic banks operate is totally absent from the analysis. The protection of property rights, the maintenance of the rule of law and control of corruption are important variables when it comes to partnership contracts. In more primitive markets, the fear of a bad reputation can ensure that an entrepreneur does not take an investment from financiers and abscond. However, in deeper and more sophisticated markets, it is important that legal and social institutions exist so that private property can be defined and contracts enforced. This is often absent in Islamic countries. In the absence of good social institutions supporting relationships based on trust, profit-and-loss sharing contracts are avoided and replaced with *murabaha* and debt-like instruments.

After four decades in existence, it seems as if Islamic finance has fallen short on offering a very different alternative to conventional finance. Nevertheless, it is clear that Islamic bankers have succeeded in developing a new industry, which is now part of the financial landscape. Whether it is faithful to Islam or not, Islamic finance is attracting more and more players, Muslim and non-Muslims alike. It could be argued that they are more interested in whether the business is profitable than the underlying compliance of the business with Islamic norms. However, Islamic finance is more likely to flourish if the legal and institutional environment is supportive of business more generally – and this is a problem in many Islamic countries. Furthermore, the total Islamisation of the financial system is no solution to the problem that some Islamic financial institutions operating in the real world do not keep within the spirit of Islam: that is an attempt to impose an ideal on an imperfect world.

References

AAOIFI (2010) *Sharia Standards*. Manama: Accounting and Auditing Organization for Islamic Financial Institutions.

Aggarwal, R. K. and Yousef, T. (2000) Islamic banks and investment financing. *Journal of Money, Credit and Banking* 32(1): 93–120.

Ayub, M. (2007) *Understanding Islamic Finance*. London: John Wiley & Sons.

Chéhata, C. (1971) *Etudes de droit musulman*. Paris: Presses Universitaires de France.

Dar, H. A. and Presley, J. R. (2000) Lack of profit loss sharing in Islamic banking: management and control imbalances. *International Journal of Business and Management Science* 2(2).

El-Gamal, M. A. (2006) *Islamic Finance: Law, Economics and Practice.* Cambridge University Press.

Godlewski, C. J., Turk, R. and Weill, L. (2014) Do the type of *sukuk* and choice of Shari'a scholar matter? IMF Working Paper WP/14/147.

Hourani, A. (1993) *Histoire des peuples arabes.* Paris: Seuil.

Khan, F. (2010) How 'Islamic' is Islamic banking? *Journal of Economic Behavior & Organization* 76: 805–20.

Kuran, T. (1993) The economic impact of Islamic fundamentalism. In *Fundamentalisms and the State: Remaking Polities, Economies, and Militance* (ed. M. E. Marty and R. S. Appleby), pp. 302–41. University of Chicago Press.

Usmani, T. M. (2002) *An Introduction to Islamic Finance.* The Hague: Kluwer Law International.

Usmani, T. M. (2008) *Sukuk and Their Contemporary Applications.* Manama: Accounting and Auditing Organization for Islamic Financial Institutions.

ABOUT THE IEA

The Institute is a research and educational charity (No. CC 235 351), limited by guarantee. Its mission is to improve understanding of the fundamental institutions of a free society by analysing and expounding the role of markets in solving economic and social problems.

The IEA achieves its mission by:

- a high-quality publishing programme
- conferences, seminars, lectures and other events
- outreach to school and college students
- brokering media introductions and appearances

The IEA, which was established in 1955 by the late Sir Antony Fisher, is an educational charity, not a political organisation. It is independent of any political party or group and does not carry on activities intended to affect support for any political party or candidate in any election or referendum, or at any other time. It is financed by sales of publications, conference fees and voluntary donations.

In addition to its main series of publications the IEA also publishes a quarterly journal, *Economic Affairs*.

The IEA is aided in its work by a distinguished international Academic Advisory Council and an eminent panel of Honorary Fellows. Together with other academics, they review prospective IEA publications, their comments being passed on anonymously to authors. All IEA papers are therefore subject to the same rigorous independent refereeing process as used by leading academic journals.

IEA publications enjoy widespread classroom use and course adoptions in schools and universities. They are also sold throughout the world and often translated/reprinted.

Since 1974 the IEA has helped to create a worldwide network of 100 similar institutions in over 70 countries. They are all independent but share the IEA's mission.

Views expressed in the IEA's publications are those of the authors, not those of the Institute (which has no corporate view), its Managing Trustees, Academic Advisory Council members or senior staff.

Members of the Institute's Academic Advisory Council, Honorary Fellows, Trustees and Staff are listed on the following page.

The Institute gratefully acknowledges financial support for its publications programme and other work from a generous benefaction by the late Professor Ronald Coase.

Other books recently published by the IEA include:

The Future of the Commons – Beyond Market Failure and Government Regulation
Elinor Ostrom et al.
Occasional Paper 148; ISBN 978-0-255-36653-3; £10.00

Redefining the Poverty Debate – Why a War on Markets Is No Substitute for a War on Poverty
Kristian Niemietz
Research Monograph 67; ISBN 978-0-255-36652-6; £12.50

The Euro – the Beginning, the Middle … and the End?
Edited by Philip Booth
Hobart Paperback 39; ISBN 978-0-255-36680-9; £12.50

The Shadow Economy
Friedrich Schneider & Colin C. Williams
Hobart Paper 172; ISBN 978-0-255-36674-8; £12.50

Quack Policy – Abusing Science in the Cause of Paternalism
Jamie Whyte
Hobart Paper 173; ISBN 978-0-255-36673-1; £10.00

Foundations of a Free Society
Eamonn Butler
Occasional Paper 149; ISBN 978-0-255-36687-8; £12.50

The Government Debt Iceberg
Jagadeesh Gokhale
Research Monograph 68; ISBN 978-0-255-36666-3; £10.00

A U-Turn on the Road to Serfdom
Grover Norquist
Occasional Paper 150; ISBN 978-0-255-36686-1; £10.00

New Private Monies – A Bit-Part Player?
Kevin Dowd
Hobart Paper 174; ISBN 978-0-255-36694-6; £10.00

From Crisis to Confidence – Macroeconomics after the Crash
Roger Koppl
Hobart Paper 175; ISBN 978-0-255-36693-9; £12.50

Advertising in a Free Society
Ralph Harris and Arthur Seldon
With an introduction by Christopher Snowdon
Hobart Paper 176; ISBN 978-0-255-36696-0; £12.50

Selfishness, Greed and Capitalism: Debunking Myths about the Free Market
Christopher Snowdon
Hobart Paper 177; ISBN 978-0-255-36677-9; £12.50

Waging the War of Ideas
John Blundell
Occasional Paper 131; ISBN 978-0-255-36684-7; £12.50

Brexit: Directions for Britain Outside the EU
Ralph Buckle, Tim Hewish, John C. Hulsman, Iain Mansfield and Robert Oulds
Hobart Paperback 178; ISBN 978-0-255-36681-6; £12.50

Flaws and Ceilings – Price Controls and the Damage They Cause
Edited by Christopher Coyne and Rachel Coyne
Hobart Paperback 179; ISBN 978-0-255-36701-1; £12.50

Scandinavian Unexceptionalism: Culture, Markets and the Failure of Third-Way Socialism
Nima Sanandaji
Readings in Political Economy 1; ISBN 978-0-255-36704-2; £10.00

Classical Liberalism – A Primer
Eamonn Butler
Readings in Political Economy 2; ISBN 978-0-255-36707-3; £10.00

Federal Britain: The Case for Decentralisation
Philip Booth
Readings in Political Economy 3; ISBN 978-0-255-36713-4; £10.00

Forever Contemporary: The Economics of Ronald Coase
Edited by Cento Veljanovski
Readings in Political Economy 4; ISBN 978-0-255-36710-3; £15.00

Power Cut? How the EU Is Pulling the Plug on Electricity Markets
Carlo Stagnaro
Hobart Paperback 180; ISBN 978-0-255-36716-5; £10.00

Policy Stability and Economic Growth – Lessons from the Great Recession
John B. Taylor
Readings in Political Economy 5; ISBN 978-0-255-36719-6; £7.50

Breaking Up Is Hard To Do: Britain and Europe's Dysfunctional Relationship
Edited by Patrick Minford and J. R. Shackleton
Hobart Paperback 181; ISBN 978-0-255-36722-6; £15.00

In Focus: The Case for Privatising the BBC
Edited by Philip Booth
Hobart Paperback 182; ISBN 978-0-255-36725-7; £12.50

Other IEA publications

Comprehensive information on other publications and the wider work of the IEA can be found at www.iea.org.uk. To order any publication please see below.

Personal customers

Orders from personal customers should be directed to the IEA:

Clare Rusbridge
IEA
2 Lord North Street
FREEPOST LON10168
London SW1P 3YZ
Tel: 020 7799 8907. Fax: 020 7799 2137
Email: sales@iea.org.uk

Trade customers

All orders from the book trade should be directed to the IEA's distributor:

NBN International (IEA Orders)
Orders Dept.
NBN International
10 Thornbury Road
Plymouth PL6 7PP
Tel: 01752 202301, Fax: 01752 202333
Email: orders@nbninternational.com

IEA subscriptions

The IEA also offers a subscription service to its publications. For a single annual payment (currently £42.00 in the UK), subscribers receive every monograph the IEA publishes. For more information please contact:

Clare Rusbridge
Subscriptions
IEA
2 Lord North Street
FREEPOST LON10168
London SW1P 3YZ
Tel: 020 7799 8907, Fax: 020 7799 2137
Email: crusbridge@iea.org.uk

Islamic Foundations of a Free Society